H

822

PINERO.A.
Two plays.

21339

CENTRAL RESERVE STOCK

C:

14

This Book
below.

FINES :—
First
Seco
After the

-4 JAN 5
13 FEB.
22 FEP
30 MA
26 J
25 NC
15 N

C0000 000 500 728

# TWO PLAYS

## BY THE SAME AUTHOR

◆

THE AMAZONS
THE BENEFIT OF THE DOUBT
THE BIG DRUM
THE CABINET MINISTER
DANDY DICK
THE ENCHANTED COTTAGE
THE FREAKS
THE GAY LORD QUEX
THE HOBBY HORSE
HIS HOUSE IN ORDER
IRIS
LADY BOUNTIFUL
LETTY
THE MAGISTRATE
MID-CHANNEL
THE MIND THE PAINT GIRL
THE NOTORIOUS MRS. EBBSMITH
PRESERVING MR. PANMURE
THE PRINCESS AND THE BUTTERFLY
THE SCHOOLMISTRESS
THE SECOND MRS. TANQUERAY
SWEET LAVENDER
THE THUNDERBOLT
THE TIMES
TRELAWNY OF THE WELLS

# TWO PLAYS

by

## ARTHUR PINERO

HESTON & ISLEWORTH DISTRICT ★ PUBLIC LIBRARIES
HOUNSLOW

LONDON

WILLIAM HEINEMANN LTD

COPYRIGHT 1930 BY ARTHUR PINERO

(All rights reserved)

CLASS 812 PIN

ACC. 21330

SHELF 1:335

First published 1930

Printed in Great Britain at
The Windmill Press,
Kingswood
Surrey

# CONTENTS

❖

HESTON & ISLEWORTH DISTRICT
HOUNSLOW
PUBLIC LIBRARIES

# FOREWORD

I WROTE *Dr. Harmer's Holidays* in 1923–24. A criminal trial—Regina *v.* Waller and others—which I witnessed at the Old Bailey as far back as November, 1892, suggested to me the main idea of the play. At that trial three men stood in the dock charged with the murder of a young doctor who up to the events which led to his death had borne an irreproachable character. The victim, dirty and dishevelled and bemused with drink, but obviously of a superior class, had been found by Waller and his associates in the bar of a public-house in the Borough, and thence led away to a blind alley nearby and there robbed and fatally maltreated. One of the accused kept watch at the mouth of the alley while his companions held the struggling man to the ground and rifled his pockets, unfortunately apply-ing too much pressure to his windpipe in the course of the transaction. A little girl—small enough to be dis-regarded—passing the alley at the time, beer-jug in hand, caught a glimpse, through the straddled legs of the guardian of the entrance, of what was going on; and her intelligently-given evidence was a considerable factor in bringing the prisoners to justice. Thus will a slight excess of confidence contribute to our undoing! The usual arguments were advanced by counsel on both sides as to what constitutes murder, what man-slaughter. Ultimately, aided by the judge, the jury

v

took a merciful view of the case and satisfied their consciences with a verdict of "manslaughter." I recollect clearly the change in the aspect and demeanour of the three pallid, drawn-faced wretches when they realised that they had escaped paying the extreme penalty. Colour returned to their ashen cheeks, their limp bodies straightened, and they shuffled about in the dock with the air of men who had just won a big bet at Epsom. The prospect of a long term of penal servitude seemed to have small terrors beside the awful dread of the gallows.

The length of the sentences, varied in degree, dealt out to these gentry I have forgotten; in fact, the period of suspension put to their activities did not much concern me. What interested me at the moment, and continued to interest me thirty years later, was the problem of the respectable young doctor—the trusted assistant of an older practitioner in the City, if I remember aright—apparently living a sober, honest and cleanly life, who met his end in such an ignoble fashion; and I set myself to the task of forging a chain of circumstances, intensifying rather than diminishing the tragedy of his death, which would, granting the premises, account naturally for that desperate, and final, fight for breath in those lone and noisome surroundings. The result, poor as it may be after so protracted a cogitation, is *Dr. Harmer's Holidays*.

*Child Man* was written last year. I call it a sedate farce because, extravagant as it is, none of its personages sits on a bandbox, nor, I submit, does anything wholly inconceivable. ("Tell me, Toole," a candid friend once asked the celebrated low-comedian—"tell me why you will persist in sitting on a bandbox in so many of your pieces." "Well, you see," replied Toole, in a confidential whisper and with his characteristic wry face, "it never fails to get a laugh.")

To what extent is it permissible for a dramatist, in publishing his play, to describe the scenes in minute detail and, after trying to help the reader to visualise the physical attributes of the characters, break up the dialogue by indicating the positions and movements of those characters and the manner in which certain speeches should be delivered? In other words, how far with propriety may an author go, in a published play, towards particularising the tone and action of his drama? Ought he to restrict himself almost entirely to dialogue and leave the rest to the reader's imagination? I have lately been scolded for overburdening my published plays with stage directions, and I confess that my stage directions have become more abundant in recent years. My excuse, if excuse is needed, is that I "stage-manage" my play as I write it, and that, having brought the thing into some sort of being, I am unable—perhaps because I am a lazy man—to retouch it. At any rate, to ask me to remodel a play, by excision or otherwise, is—an ancient simile—like asking a mother to alter the shape of her baby's nose or the colour of its eyes.

What are the objections urged against the insertion of stage directions in the published work? In the first place, we are told that a play should not encroach upon the form and province of the novel; in the second place, that stage directions impede the reader's progress and spoil his enjoyment, and, further, that the planning of the scenery, the designing of the decorations, and the action—*i.e.*, the " business "—of the play, apart from the mere coming on and going off of the characters, and with the possible exception of such a vital incident as the administration by the hero of a knock-out blow to the villain's chin, have nothing to do with the author at all and should properly be left to the invention of that modern excrescence of the theatre—if I may be pardoned the expression— the " producer." And finally it is contended that the interpolation of stage directions blurs the literary appearance of the published work, making it resemble the well-thumbed prompt-book of, let us say, the popular provincial melodrama of *Woman's Wiles, or The Assistant Bank Manager's Downfall*. This last argument, I suspect, is particularly acceptable to the author who has but a nodding acquaintance with the technique of the stage. At all events he avoids the risk of his play not looking like " literature."

Now, why should there not be a likeness between the novel and the published play? If stage directions are to be held as trespassing upon the form of a novel, a chapter of a novel made up in a large measure of dialogue is equally an encroachment on the form of a play. In some novels the author, when it suits his purpose, will drop for the moment the purely narrative

form and give us dialogue in which each speech, as
in a play, is headed with the name of the speaker.
These instances are rare, but they do occur, and meet
with no reproof. I am for freedom all round. And if
it be tedious to read an ample description in a play of
a room, a garden, a man and a woman and their movements and gestures in talking to one another, surely it
is just as tedious to read such matter in a novel. (It
often *is*, but that is beside the question.) I don't, of
course, defend in a published play the old-fashioned
stage directions full of technicalities understood only
by theatre folk—" enter Brown L.U.E., exit Smith
D.R." (" L.U.E." signifying Left Upper Entrance and
" D.R." Down Right). Nor do I advocate the method
employed by some serious writers in introducing a
character of whom the reader knows nothing—" Robinson has the look of a man who has an aunt living at
Penge," for example. This may impress the reader
as a piece of subtlety; but it is sham drama, whatever
may be its relation to literature.

What I do advocate, with the presumptuousness, and
the prejudices, of an old theatrical hand, is that the
dramatist should in a practical way stage-manage his
play as he goes along, describing fully in his manuscript,
in simple, decent English—here I leave myself open to
attack—his scenes, his characters and the action of his
drama, and so prevent a " producer " from coming
betwixt the wind and his nobility and pushing him to
the wall. If, in addition, he can subsequently get upon
the stage and expound his views, so much the better;

if he lacks the necessary assurance, the aplomb, to do this, a " producer " may be called in to act as interpreter, which is that functionary's real job. But I venture positively to assert that the dramatist who does not stage-manage his play, at least with his pen, performs only part of his task, and that to suffer another to clothe the bare bones of his work in garments not of his own choosing is tantamount to an admission of incapacity.

But all this is no palliation of the fault of bewildering the reader of the published book with a superfluity of stage directions, and if I err in this respect—to borrow Mr. Gillbanks' favourite phrase—I apologise. To my mind, however, a play, in any shape, is never easily digestible, which perhaps is the reason why fewer plays are published than novels. The fact is that a novel can be read, while a play needs to be studied. I speak of great plays, not of those included in this volume.

A. P.

*London: October,* 1929.

# DR. HARMER'S HOLIDAYS

### A CONTRAST
### IN NINE SCENES

# THE PERSONS OF THE PLAY

WALTER HARMER, M.D.

JOHN MACGILL, M.R.C.S., L.R.C.P. (*a retired practitioner*).

REVD. OSWALD BIRKETT (*Minister of the Laleham Road Congregational Chapel*).

PERCY CRICKMAY.

GEORGE KELK.

ALFRED GORHAM.

MRS. NETHERCLIFF (*Harmer's landlady*).

ELSIE SPEED (*her niece*).

LILIAN DIPPLE.

FLORENCE PORTCH.

IDA (*Mrs. Nethercliff's servant*).

*The story of the play covers a period of twelve months.*

3

# THE SCENES

# THE FIRST SCENE

*A room such as one would be likely to find in a sub-urban villa of a superior class. The decorations are bright, but in good taste, and the effect of the entire scene is one of neatness and cheerfulness.*

*In the wall at the back there is a set of folding-doors with four leaves. Only the right-centre leaf, which opens into the adjoining room, is used. In the right-hand wall is the fireplace. The grate is empty, but a brass coal-scuttle filled with pots of growing flowers stands on the hearth. Opposite the fireplace, but a little nearer to the back wall, there is a door of ordinary size. When this door is opened, a passage is seen which may be supposed to run from a small hall at the nearer end of the passage to the kitchen-quarters at the other end.*

*Near the fireplace, directly facing the spectator, stands a capacious and comfortably upholstered settee. At the end of the settee farthest from the fireplace is a small table with a tin of tobacco, an array of pipes, a box of cigarettes and a bowl of matches upon it, and fronting the fireplace is an arm-chair of a light kind moving easily upon its castors. Another, and a larger, arm-chair stands at the nearer side of the fireplace, close to the wall and facing, at an angle, the settee.*

*Slightly to the left of the middle of the room*

7

*there is a round table of medium size, and on the farther side of it is a small chair; and on the extreme left of the room, nearer to the spectator, and at a short distance from the wall, there is an oblong table set obliquely towards the left-hand corner of the room. Before this table, its back to the spectator, is another small chair, and on the table are a blotting-pad, an inkstand, a date-box—showing the date of the thirty-first of July—and other accessories of a writing-table.*

*Against the left-hand wall, on the nearer side of the door, are a cottage-piano and a music-stool; against the wall at the back, on the left of the folding-doors, is a bureau-bookcase; and on the right of the folding-doors, also against the wall, there is a semi-circular table laden with odd books and magazines. A jardinière with gay flowers in it stands against the left-centre division of the folding-doors; there is a smaller jardinière against the right-hand wall at the nearer side of the fireplace; and other articles of furniture—such as an additional chair or two—fill spaces not specifically provided for in this description.*

*Hanging on the walls are a few pictures—engravings of the Landseer type—and a couple of pieces of needlework in frames.*

*A lamp stands on the writing-table, and there is an electric sconce on each side of the fireplace and the folding-doors, but the light in the room is that of a fine afternoon in summer.*

*The door on the left is open.*

*(Note: Throughout, " right " and " left " are the
spectators' right and left, not the actor's.)*

[*Mrs. Nethercliff, a good-looking, elderly woman
in a simple but becoming gown, is laying a
crochet-bordered cloth upon the round table.
Presently Ida, a neatly dressed young maidservant, enters at the open door. She comes
from the farther end of the passage and is
carrying a tray on which are tea-cups, plates,
et cætera, for two persons.*

IDA. [*To Mrs. Nethercliff.*] The front-door bell's just
rung, ma'am.

MRS. NETHERCLIFF. [*Taking the tray from her and
setting it on the table.*] I expect that *is* Dr. MacGill,
Ida.

IDA. [*Going into the passage and turning to her left.*]
Yes, ma'am; shouldn't be surprised.

MRS. NETHERCLIFF. [*Listening as she arranges the
plates and some small knives on the table, and then raising her voice.*] Come in, doctor.

MACGILL. [*Out of sight.*] A'ha! [*Chuckling.*] Ha, ha,
ha! [*MacGill, a genial, grey-haired man of between
sixty and sixty-five, bustles in with Ida at his heels.*]
Am I late?

MRS. NETHERCLIFF. [*Going to him.*] Not a bit.

MACGILL. [*To Ida, giving her his hat and stick.*]
How're you, Ida?

9

IDA. [*Beaming.*] Very well, thank you, sir; hope you're the same.

MACGILL. [*As Ida withdraws and closes the door—folding both Mrs. Nethercliff's hands in his own.*] And you, my dear?

MRS. NETHERCLIFF. I should be all the better for seeing you a little oftener. One would think you lived at Hongkong instead of at Balham.

MACGILL. Don't bully me. [*Pulling off his gloves as he moves to the fireplace.*] A susceptible old widower daren't trust himself in the society of a charming widow more than once in a way.

MRS. NETHERCLIFF. [*Laughing.*] For shame! Be quiet!

MACGILL. Ha, ha, ha! [*Pocketing his gloves.*] Where's Harmer?

MRS. NETHERCLIFF. Run out to see a patient; he'll be back in a few minutes. [*Pushing the arm-chair which faces the fireplace to the right-hand side of the round table, so that it fronts the table.*] In spite of my charms, you're going to have the courage, it appears, to trust yourself to me for three weeks or a month. You've promised to do August for him, Dr. Harmer tells me.

MACGILL. Yes. [*Glancing at the tea-table.*] He and I are settling matters over a cup of your excellent tea.

MRS. NETHERCLIFF. Awfully sweet and kind of you.

MACGILL. Gammon! Couldn't refuse. That ass Jedwin, who usually helps him, has fallen down stairs and smashed his knee-pan.

MRS. NETHERCLIFF. [*Nodding.*] I know. But it's an ill wind—! You're coming in to-morrow, aren't you?

MACGILL. In the morning, madam, by your leave.

[*Elsie opens the door and enters, carrying a plate of bread-and-butter and a silver basket with cakes in it. She is a pale, pretty, slim girl in a dainty white frock.*

MRS. NETHERCLIFF. [*Taking the basket and the bread-and-butter from her.*] Here's Elsie.

MACGILL. [*Holding out his arms to Elsie.*] Bless my soul, what an improvement!

ELSIE. [*Going to him shyly.*] Good afternoon, Dr. MacGill.

MACGILL. [*His hands on her shoulders.*] Why, Elsie, you've got the colour of a milkmaid, and you're as fat as a pig!

ELSIE. [*With rather a doleful smile.*] A very sickly milkmaid, I'm afraid, and a pig in a decline.

MACGILL. Nonsense, child; rubbish!

ELSIE. [*Eagerly.*] Do you really think I'm looking stronger, Dr. MacGill; do you really?

MRS. NETHERCLIFF. [*Who has put the bread-and-butter and the basket of cakes upon the table—joining them.*] Of course Dr. MacGill thinks so, Elsie dear, or he wouldn't speak as he does.

ELSIE. [*To MacGill, brightening.*] Anyhow, I'm to be in *your* care for the next three or four weeks; that's a nice responsibility for you. [*Slipping her hand in his.*] I *am* glad you are to be Dr. Harmer's *locum* this year, Dr. MacGill.

MACGILL. [*Patting her hand.*] Ha, ha! You wait! You may find that I'm stricter with you than Harmer.

ELSIE. Impossible! You couldn't be.

MACGILL. Dragging a rusty old fellow out of his retirement in this way! Infamous! I'll revenge myself by making you still fatter—cramming you as they do the baby chickens we eat at the West End rest'rongs.

ELSIE. [*Releasing her hand and making a piteous face.*] Oh, Dr. MacGill!

MRS. NETHERCLIFF. [*Gently but reprovingly.*] Elsie——!

ELSIE. All right; I'll be good. [*To MacGill.*] I mustn't spoil your chat with auntie.

MRS. NETHERCLIFF. [*As Elsie goes to the door.*] Make the tea directly you hear Dr. Harmer come in, Elsie.

ELSIE. Yes, aunt.

[*She goes out, shutting the door behind her, and then, after a moment's pause, MacGill seats himself upon the settee.*

MACGILL. [*With a slight change of tone.*] What does Harmer say about her?

MRS. NETHERCLIFF. [*By the chair on the right of the round table.*] He's encouraging. He believes that in two or three years' time she'll have her health completely.

MACGILL. What's her age?

MRS. NETHERCLIFF. [*Turning the chair towards MacGill.*] Eighteen last January.

MACGILL. [*Cheeringly.*] Well! If that's his opinion——

MRS. NETHERCLIFF. [*Sighing faintly as she sits.*] I

wish it could be sooner, naturally. There are special reasons in poor Elsie's case—but I won't bother you with *them*.

MACGILL. Anæmia is a beastly obstinate business. You must be patient.

MRS. NETHERCLIFF. I am—oh, and grateful; grateful to Providence. What I should do now without these two to fuss and fidget over I can't imagine.

MACGILL. Two——?

MRS. NETHERCLIFF. Dr. Harmer and my dear little orphan niece. I declare I'm nearly as fond of one as the other.

MACGILL. Harmer! Get along with you; I shall be jealous!

MRS. NETHERCLIFF. [*Smiling.*] You've only yourself to blame. It was you who advised him to set up in my house, and brought us together.

MACGILL. By Jove, so it was!

MRS. NETHERCLIFF. Five years ago! It seems yesterday!

MACGILL. I told him that sharing a high-class villa with an estimable lady who is the widow of a local practitioner would inspire as much confidence as having an establishment of his own; and so it has proved, eh?

MRS. NETHERCLIFF. Yes, indeed. He was a success almost from the start, I'm proud to say.

MACGILL. [*Smiling back at her.*] I admit, a likeable chap. There! Does that please you? Most likeable.

MRS. NETHERCLIFF. He's more than likeable; he's adorable.

13

MACGILL. [*Hazily.*] I met him first—where did I first meet Harmer?——

MRS. NETHERCLIFF. There's some quality in him, apart from his being a clever doctor, that attracts people enormously. If the lawn-mower's out of order, or there's a hole in the copper-kettle, they consult him about it!

MACGILL. He must have impressed *me* favourably even five years ago; that's evident. I'm delighted to be able to do him a service. Where's he off to for his holiday?

MRS. NETHERCLIFF. [*Dryly.*] Ha! You must ask *him* that. [*Shifting in her chair.*] It may surprise you, but I haven't the least idea.

MACGILL. [*Showing no surprise.*] Keeps it to himself?

MRS. NETHERCLIFF. As though he's frightened I'll rush round to the neighbours and gossip! [*Rising and replacing the chair at the table.*] It's always been the same, ever since he came to me. His holidays are the one thing he vexes me over—the mystery he makes of them! [*Walking away.*] Elsie and I have ceased to mention the subject in his presence.

MACGILL. [*Mildly.*] Quite wise, if he'd rather not discuss it.

MRS. NETHERCLIFF. Discuss fiddlesticks! [*Halting at the farther side of the writing-table and, in a fret, tidying the objects on the table.*] I can understand his wanting to keep his whereabouts a secret from people who'd be likely to worry him; but why conceal his movements from *me*—his mother, as I call myself? It's too annoying. [*MacGill rises and slowly wanders across to her.*] Once a year, for three weeks or a month, to die out—that's what it practically amounts to—to die out of the lives of those who are devoted to him; never to write a letter or a post-card, or supply us with an address where he can be written *to,* and where letters can be forwarded; never to give the smallest sign or token that he's still above ground! It's most inconsiderate; it's unfeeling; it's——[*checking herself and laying her hand gently on MacGill's coat-sleeve*] you won't tell him I've been complaining, will you? This is strictly between ourselves?

MACGILL. Of course, of course, of course.

MRS. NETHERCLIFF. [*Fanning herself with her hand.*] Phew! [*Going to the smoking-table and there repeating the tidying process.*] Ha, ha! Forgive the slight rise in the temperature, old friend.

MACGILL. [*Soothingly.*] It doesn't strike me that there's much " mystery " in Harmer's behaviour——

MRS. NETHERCLIFF. [*With a shrug.*] Doesn't it!

MACGILL. To some men—men who are keen on their job—it's vital to cut the painter occasionally; chuck all thought of everything and everybody connected with the shop. [*Moving a few steps towards her.*] Harmer looks as if he needed a break badly.

MRS. NETHERCLIFF. [*Facing him—expressively.*] He'll look far worse, poor boy, *after* the break, unless this holiday differs from his former ones.

MACGILL. [*Opening his eyes at her.*] What on earth d'ye mean?

MRS. NETHERCLIFF. That's what upsets me so! I mean that he'll come back to us obviously no better for his change—shockingly ill, in fact; and if I forget my resolution not to question him, and try to glean where he's been, he'll pretend not to hear me, or start another topic quickly, or make an excuse to get away from me; and I'm left, distressed beyond bearing, to nurse him and cosset him and put him on his feet again! [*Going to the fireplace.*] And you wonder at my using the word " mystery "!

MACGILL. [*Following her—knitting his brows.*] When I saw him yesterday he said he'd just sent his luggage to Paddington, but that he hadn't made up his mind where he'd book to.

MRS. NETHERCLIFF. [*Fingering her bangles impatiently.*] Oh, yes, that's the usual procedure—Paddington, or Waterloo, or Victoria!

MACGILL. Suggests a seaside holiday—Devonshire or Cornwall?

MRS. NETHERCLIFF. Suggests a flight to the moon! [*Tapping her foot upon the floor.*] This year, last year, the year before; as I tell you, his proceedings never vary. Yesterday his luggage went to Paddington; to-night, at ten o'clock, Elsie and I will bid him good-bye, and go to our beds; to-morrow morning, when we come down to breakfast, he'll have vanished. Then—a blank; and ultimately a message on the telephone: " don't lock-up to-night; I'm coming home." And next morning we'll find him at the breakfast-table, with a thin, white face and black rims round his eyes, opening a pile of letters with shaky hands. [*Her mouth quivering.*] It's maddening, John MacGill; it's maddening!

MACGILL. [*Touching her arm.*] Tsch, tsch, tsch! Perhaps a great deal of it is your fancy. [*Forcing a laugh.*] Ha, ha, ha! You women——!

MRS. NETHERCLIFF. [*Quickly.*] Ah, no; don't joke! [*Motioning him to the settee.*] Listen. [*They sit side by side and she again lays her hand on his sleeve.*] I—I have a theory.

MACGILL. As to——?

MRS. NETHERCLIFF. As to how Dr. Harmer spends his summer holiday.

MACGILL. *What's* your theory?

MRS. NETHERCLIFF. [*Intensely.*] Recollect, *I know him.* Nothing is so penetrating as affection. He's the most self-sacrificing, charitable creature in the world. None of his patients, for instance, who are hard-up ever get an account from him. He'd beggar himself to do a generous act. He's good—Walter Harmer is; good through and through!

MACGILL. [*A trifle techily.*] Yes, yes——

MRS. NETHERCLIFF. [*In a hushed voice.*] My theory is that he doesn't go away at all, not to any distance.

MACGILL. [*A little startled.*] No?

MRS. NETHERCLIFF. No; he spends his holiday in working in some low part of London among the poor. [*Hitting her knee with her fist.*] I'd swear I'm right.

MACGILL. [*Blinking.*] But—but—but—er——?

MRS. NETHERCLIFF. His sending his trunk, full of

his smart clothes, to the station—a blind; a trick to silence us—to stop an outcry from Elsie and me! [*Throwing her head up.*] Ha! Good men are always bunglers at deceiving; but you'd scarcely credit he could overlook *one* precaution!

MACGILL. What's that?

MRS. NETHERCLIFF. Does he think I'm such a ninny as not to notice! When his luggage is brought back to the house, *there are no labels on it,* and no trace of there having been any. It's as clean as when the railway-van fetched it.

MACGILL. [*Knitting his brows again.*] Really?

MRS. NETHERCLIFF. [*Grasping MacGill's arm.*] But the most conclusive proof that there's something in my theory is this: *he burns every scrap of clothing he returns in.*

MACGILL. Burns—his clothing——?

MRS. NETHERCLIFF. As if it's dirty—contagious. [*Restraining a slight movement from MacGill.*] Joe Carling, the gardener, lights a bonfire once a week at the bottom of the kitchen-garden, and while Joe's at his dinner, Dr. Harmer, with a huge bundle under his arm —[*listening*] hark! [*She rises and goes to the folding-doors and puts her ear to the crack in the centre. Then she turns to MacGill, who has also risen.*] He's home. I hear him in the consulting-room.

> [*The right-centre leaf of the folding doors is opened by Harmer, who enters with a bright smile. He is a man of four-and-thirty, and his hair is already whitening at the temples, but his face*

*is young, though somewhat careworn, and his
manner is engagingly boyish.*

HARMER. [*Closing the door.*] Ah—! [*Advancing to
MacGill and shaking hands with him vigorously.*] Sorry.
Have I kept you long?

MACGILL. [*Heartily.*] Not long enough. I've been
having a splendid jaw with my old friend there.

HARMER. I'll be bound you have! [*To Mrs. Nethercliff, who is now at the door on the left.*] Tea, Mrs.
Nethercliff darling!

MRS. NETHERCLIFF. [*Smiling at him fondly and
hurrying out, leaving the door ajar.*] In a second.

HARMER. [*As she disappears—almost embracing Mac-
Gill.*] MacGill, you're a trump—a regular trump to
throw yourself into the breach like this. I wish I knew
how to thank you.

MACGILL. P'tah! P'sh! I intend to enjoy myself—
sit in the garden and smoke, and play cards with the
ladies. There won't be much else to do at this time o'
year.

HARMER. No; but it's a comfort to me all the same to
leave a man of your sort in charge here—a real comfort——

MACGILL. Shut up! Spare my blushes!

HARMER. [*Holding the lapel of MacGill's jacket.*]
You see, MacGill, when I take my holiday, I *rest*; I
allow nothing, and nobody, to disturb me. I rest. I'm
as dead to the world as a kid asleep in a perambulator.

MACGILL. [*Eyeing him attentively.*] Capital system,
if you can follow it.

HARMER. Oh, you can follow it, if you're firm. [*Placing a finger on a button of MacGill's waistcoat.*] Don't let on to a soul where you're staying—that's the recipe; not to your dearest pal. What happens in your absence —happens; as it would happen, the odds are, if you were on the spot. It's the only way, sir. I've done the other thing, and the mere sight of a postman or a telegraph-boy gave me the belly-ache. I assure you it's the only way.

MACGILL. Never had the pluck to put the system into practice myself; but I agree. [*Emphatically, still with an eye on Harmer.*] *Rest*—total, absolute rest——!

[*Elsie, coming from the farther end of the passage, pushes open the door on the left and enters, carrying, on a small tray, a silver teapot and hot-water jug and a cut-glass dish of jam.*

HARMER. [*Meeting her at the tea-table.*] Hallo, Elsie!

ELSIE. [*Demurely.*] Hallo!

HARMER. Here's Dr. MacGill.

ELSIE. [*Standing the teapot and jug upon the tea-tray.*] Dr. MacGill and I have exchanged civilities.

HARMER. [*Taking the dish of jam from her and putting it on the table.*] Hardly seen you all day. How goes it, old girl?

ELSIE. Oh, I'm in the wildest spirits.

HARMER. Are you! What over?

ELSIE. At the prospect of Dr. MacGill moving in to-morrow.

MACGILL. [*Rubbing his hands together.*] A'ha! Ha, ha, ha!

20

HARMER. [*To MacGill.*] Good for *you*, MacGill.

ELSIE. [*On her way to the door.*] Yes, it will be such a relief to have a competent G.P. in the Avenue.

HARMER. [*Making a dash at her.*] You cat!

ELSIE. [*Flying out of the room.*] Ha, ha, ha, ha——!

HARMER. [*Half in the passage, calling after her warningly.*] Don't run, Elsie! Steady, dear; steady! [*Sobered, he closes the door and turns to MacGill.*] Poor mite! You'll keep a sharp eye on her, won't you?

MACGILL. [*With a nod.*] Trust *me*.

HARMER. Sad she should be such a weakling. [*Strolling to the tea-table.*] Heaven knows when her marriage will come off!

MACGILL. Marriage——?

HARMER. She's engaged—provisionally engaged—to a man in the neighbourhood—quite a decent fellow according to his lights——

MACGILL. *Provisionally* engaged——?

HARMER. [*By the chair facing the tea-tray.*] Well, his conscience forbids him to marry an invalid—a young woman whose state of health might interfere with the discharge of his duties.

MACGILL. [*Hotly.*] Good God! Who the devil's the brute?

HARMER. Name of Birkett—[*with a jerk of his head*] minister of the chapel in Laleham Road——

MACGILL. [*In disgust.*] Chapel!

HARMER. I suppose these dissenting parsons have a sterner sense of duty to their flock than our Church of England chaps.

MACGILL. Duty be damned! A ruffian!

HARMER. [*Laughing at MacGill's vehemence.*] Ha, ha, ha! [*Seating himself at the tea-table.*] They fell in love at a bazaar, or a tennis crowd—some jamboree of that kind. [*Lightly.*] Come and sit down.

MACGILL. [*Sitting in the chair on the right of the table—witheringly.*] In love—*he!* When I married my poor dear wife, she had a spine that was as crooked as a winding river.

HARMER. [*Pouring out the tea.*] I confess we're only moderately happy about it. A nonconformist nephew-in-law is a bitter pill for the aunt to swallow.

MACGILL. [*Growling.*] Bitter as gall, I should say.

HARMER. However, it may come to nothing. Milk and sugar?

MACGILL. Milk, thank'yer; no sugar.

HARMER. [*Pouring milk into one of the cups and then passing the cup to MacGill.*] Don't allude to the affair; it's rather a sore point.

MACGILL. Not I.

HARMER. [*Glancing at the things on the table.*] Bread-and-butter. Jam—strawberry, isn't it? Cakes in that basket. [*Pouring milk into the other cup.*] Help yourself, MacGill.

MACGILL. [*Spooning a little jam on to a plate and taking a slice of bread-and-butter.*] Have you made out that list of cases you promised to let me have, Harmer?

HARMER. [*Replenishing the tea-pot.*] It's on my table in the consulting-room. We'll go through it together by-and-by, shall we?

MACGILL. [*Spreading the jam upon his bread-and-butter.*] Certainly.

HARMER. [*Taking a slice of bread-and-butter.*] There are two or three pets of mine I want you to look after particularly. [*Eating.*] Mrs. Flinders—the next avenue to this—wonderful old lady—chronic bronchitis. [*Repeating the name clearly.*] Mrs. Flinders.

MACGILL. [*With his mouth full.*] I'll remember.

HARMER. Robinson, too—Cyril Robinson—"Ingleside," Frogmore Vale—subject to slight attacks of angina. He has all the usual remedies in the house, but you might call and make his acquaintance.

MACGILL. I will.

HARMER. But we'll talk about 'em later. [*Taking another slice of bread-and-butter.*] That jam good?

MACGILL. [*Passing the jam to Harmer.*] First-rate. [*Drinking.*] Well, I'll endeavour to carry-on on your lines, Harmer, though I hope fervently I shan't be asked to patch copper-kettles, or mend lawn-mowers.

HARMER. [*Puzzled.*] Lawn-mowers — copper-kettles—? What *are* you driving at?

MACGILL. [*Chuckling as he empties his cup.*] I gather from Mrs. Nethercliff that your patients don't confine themselves to consulting you about their bodily ailments. [*Handing his cup to Harmer.*] Trouble you.

HARMER. [*Pouring out another cup of tea for MacGill.*] Ha, ha! That wicked woman has been telling tales out of school, has she?

MACGILL. Been singing your praises loudly.

HARMER. She *will* make a hero of me, the old dear.

She's incorrigible. [*Returning MacGill's cup to him.*] But it's the truth; a lot of 'em do come to me for advice on more-or-less non-professional matters. [*Sipping his own tea.*] I can't think why; but they do.

MACGILL. [*Drinking again.*] I'll tell you why: because you're so devilish good-natured and self-denying, Harmer.

HARMER. Oh, tosh!

MACGILL. [*Gruffly.*] It isn't often I compliment a man to his face; but I honestly believe you deserve to have a big bookay thrown you. [*Emptying his cup again with a gulp and rising.*] May I smoke my pipe?

HARMER. [*Whose expression has suddenly grown overcast.*] Rather! [*Pointing to the smoking-table.*] Baccy—Paragon Mixture——

MACGILL. [*Producing an ancient brier and going to the table.*] Thank'yer.

HARMER. [*After a short silence, during which Mac-Gill studies the label on the tobacco-tin—speaking in a constrained, hesitating voice.*] I—I'll give you an example, MacGill, of the—the extraordinary disclosures one has to listen to. Extraordinary! [*He puts his cup down, glances furtively at MacGill—who is now sniffing the contents of the tin—and draws his hand painfully across his forehead, as if to clear his brain.*] I—I don't want to bore you——

MACGILL. [*Loading his pipe.*] You won't bore me. Go ahead.

HARMER. [*Still speaking in a laboured way but gradually recovering his usual manner.*] Some weeks ago a man turned up here and sent in word that he'd like to see me. It was in the afternoon, during my consulting hours, and I had him in—a well-dressed fellow, about my own age—four or five-and-thirty—pleasant-looking —refined—decidedly prepossessing; in all respects— outwardly, at any rate—what old-fashioned people would call a gentleman. He wouldn't give his name, for very good reasons—[*half turning to MacGill, who, with his back to Harmer, is trying ineffectually to strike a match—almost angrily*] can't you get a light?

MACGILL. [*Succeeding.*] That's it! [*He lights his pipe and settles himself comfortably on the settee. Until MacGill speaks, Harmer, his clenched hands resting on the tea-table, sits staring into space.*] Jolly nice to-bacco.

HARMER. [*Rousing himself.*] Eh—? Oh, yes; A 1.

MACGILL. [*Puffing away contentedly.*] Your visitor declined to give his name——?

HARMER. He didn't decline to give it; he—er—begged me not to ask it. He said he was related to some former patients of mine, and that he'd heard through them that I—er——

MACGILL. That you're handy at mending lawn-mowers and copper-kettles. Ha, ha!

HARMER. Ha, ha! Exactly. [*Rising and going to the smoking-table and taking a cigarette.*] Now, bear in mind, MacGill, my description of the fellow—clothes spick-and-span, a fresh appearance, clear eye and complexion, and a voice and style that could belong only to a man who's well-bred and who mixes with decent folk.

25

[*Lighting his cigarette.*] And before he'd been with me five minutes he'd launched out into a confession that would have made your hair stand on end, if you weren't proof against horrors of one kind or another.

MACGILL. Drink—drugs——?

HARMER. Neither—habitually. I've told you—a clear eye and skin——

MACGILL. Occasionally?

HARMER. [*Nodding.*] At intervals. At intervals—once a year perhaps—he'll slink away from his wholesome surroundings—where he's regarded as a model of rectitude—and abandon himelf to a course of utter depravity.

MACGILL. [*Tossing his head knowingly.*] Ah!

HARMER. Yes, but as a rule the vices of such persons are normal; [*inspecting the lighted end of his cigarette*] this chap's aberrations are *not*. No silks and satins and gaudy accessories for *him,* with the conventional champagne in the lady's boudoir! The individual I speak of dives into the foulest quarter of London he can find—the heart of the Borough, or east of Aldgate Pump, among the Chinks; and there for a term he'll swelter and soak, living, as I say, the most bestial life conceivable. [*Sitting in the chair on the right of the round table, first turning it so that it partly faces MacGill.*] My dear MacGill, he favoured me with details that would have revolted even a Thames-side police magistrate.

MACGILL. [*Not greatly moved by the narration.*] Single man?

HARMER. Yes.

26

MACGILL. I've met with similar cases. [*Shortly.*] Form of madness.

HARMER. Of course. But a madness accompanied by a dreadful sanity. There's where the tragedy comes in.

MACGILL. In the revulsion that follows the bouts?

HARMER. Quite so; [*leaning back in his chair and, with a tense face, blowing rings of smoke*] in the revulsion, the repentance, the effort on the part of the miserable wretch to cleanse himself. And then, the good resolutions, the frantic prayers at the bedside, and the conviction, as month after month slips by—the conviction that at last—at last!—the abominable appetite is dead and done for!

MACGILL. But no go!

HARMER. No! [*Carefully depositing the remains of his cigarette on the plate at his elbow.*] As you remark, no go.

MACGILL. Low hog! What the deuce did he want to bother *you* for? [*Sarcastically.*] Bottle o' med'cine?

HARMER. [*Sitting upright and slowly rubbing his knees.*] He came to me, MacGill, simply for relief.

MACGILL. Relief?

HARMER. The relief of telling his story——

MACGILL. Pretty story!

HARMER. [*Drawing a deep breath.*] The relief of putting his struggles—his sufferings—into words. [*With a gesture of helplessness.*] God Almighty—! [*He gets to his feet and moves about the room aimlessly. At this point MacGill's suspicions are aroused for the first time, and, his jaw dropping, he observes Harmer with amaze-*

*ment.*] God Almighty, MacGill, haven't you any sympathy—not a spark—for a fellow-creature who is in the clutch of an evil fate, and who cries out for a little pity—cries out in his anguish for a little pity! [*Halting, but not noticing MacGill.*] A fellow-creature! There are thousands—millions—in this terrible world who are cursed—enslaved—if not precisely in the same way, in a way that's akin to it; who, deep down in their souls, as it were, love to walk along beautiful country roads, and worship under the arches of green trees, and who are tapped on the shoulder by an unseen force and dragged off to wallow in the slime of the ditches! [*Sitting at the writing-table and, with his elbows on the table, digging his fingers into his hair.*]. Ha, ha! Why, Birkett, round the corner—Elsie's beau—the nonconformist parson—*he* wouldn't put on a more sanctified air than you do! [*Seizing a paper-knife and stabbing at the blotting-pad.*] You've missed your tip, MacGill— you ought to have been a clergyman, not a doctor; [*his voice dying away*] that's what *you* ought to have been —a clergyman—not a—doctor——!

[*MacGill has risen and crossed slowly and silently to Harmer. He is now standing near the writing-table, looking down upon him.*

MACGILL. [*Almost inaudibly.*] H—H—Harmer——?

[*There is a pause, and then Harmer, regaining command over himself, calmly lays down the paper-knife and rises with a smile.*

HARMER. [*Giving MacGill a gentle shaking.*] You— old—flint! [*Winningly.*] Dashed if I'll confide another of my odd experiences to you as long as I live! [*Stepping briskly to the folding-doors, and there turning to MacGill.*] Shall we run through that list now? It won't take two minutes.

MACGILL. [*Perplexed.*] Yes—yes——

HARMER. [*Opening the leaf of the folding-doors.*] And we'll have a stroll on the Common afterwards, shall we?

MACGILL. [*Joining Harmer.*] Yes.

HARMER. [*Slapping him on the back playfully.*] Ha, ha, ha! Ungrateful of me to scold you——!

[*Harmer pushes MacGill before him, and they go into the consulting-room.*

# THE SECOND SCENE

*The outside of the ground-floor of Mrs. Nethercliff's house, viewed from the front. In the centre is the door, which opens into the hall and is on the ground level, and on each side of the door there is a bay-window, the window on the right being the window of Harmer's sitting-room.*

*The character of the house as now shown is that of a detached villa of moderate size—the sort of villa that is approached by an inclosed carriage-drive and has a fairly large garden at the back.*

*It is night-time and the greater part of the house is in semi-darkness. The door alone is clearly visible, owing to a light, checkered by the shadow of a tree, cast by a street-lamp in the road beyond the carriage-drive.*

*[The door is opened stealthily and Harmer comes out. He is wearing a thin overcoat with the collar turned up and a soft felt hat drawn down over his brows, and he carries a smallish, much-worn leather bag. He shuts the door as noiselessly as possible, presses it with his hand to assure himself that it is secure, and then— tiptoeing to avoid crunching the gravel path— creeps away.*

# THE THIRD SCENE

*A small room on an upper floor of a house in a narrow
court in the Borough. In the wall at the back, a
little to the right of the centre, is the door. The
door opens into the room and when open reveals a
dark and dismal landing. A latch-lock and a bolt
are on the door, and on the outer side of the door
there is a knocker. In the wall on the right is a
sash-window, the lower sash being partly raised,
and seen dimly through a torn and discoloured
"lace" curtain is a row of similarly squalid houses.
A piece of old sacking, used at night as a substitute
for a blind, hangs from a nail in the window-frame.*

*In the left-hand wall, near to the spectator, is
the fireplace. The grate is empty, but a gas-ring
stands on the hearth with a blackened tin-kettle
on it; and on the floor at the farther side of the fireplace there are a few lumps of coal in a ramshackle
scuttle. Some ornaments, mostly broken, of the
kind sold at a twopenny bazaar, adorn the mantelpiece. Above the mantelpiece, in a paltry frame,
is a smoke-stained oleograph of an ideally beautiful maiden gazing heavenward, and by the side of
the mantelpiece there is a single-light gas-bracket
which has lost its globe.*

*About half-way between the door and the left-
hand wall, standing against the wall at the back
with its head to the wall, is a rusty iron bedstead.*

*A tattered patchwork coverlet hides the blankets and sheets, but a couple of grimy pillows are outside the coverlet. At the foot of the bed, a portion of a garment peeping out from under its lid, is a battered old trunk, and between the bed and the left-hand wall there is a painted chest of drawers which also serves as a washstand. On it are a ewer and basin of a hideous pattern, a jam-pot with a tooth-brush in it, and other toilet necessaries. Over the chest of drawers hangs a cracked mirror, and between the chest of drawers and the left-hand wall a soiled towel dangles on a rickety towel-horse.*

*On the other side of the bed is an orange-box turned up on end on which are a tin candlestick and a box of matches, and between the orange-box and the door Harmer's jacket and waistcoat and his overcoat and hat are hanging from some hooks attached to the wall. There is another row of hooks on the wall on the right of the door, and on these hooks, partially concealed by a chintz curtain of a design which time has almost obliterated, hang some articles of feminine attire. Also attached to the wall on the right of the door is a slot-meter, and pinned to the wall on either side of the window are some coloured prints such as are a feature of the Christmas numbers of the illustrated journals.*

*A decrepit wicker-work arm-chair, showing signs that it was once upholstered in bright plush, stands at the farther side of the fireplace, and on the right of the bed, at the nearer end, is a wooden chair turned towards the bed. Thrown over the back of this chair is a rag of a dressing-gown, and on the floor, not far off, there is a pair of woman's slippers.*

*Standing out in the room, but at no great distance from the window, is an oblong deal-table, set obliquely with its farther end to the right-hand corner of the room, and on each side of the table is a chair of the same sort as the one by the bed. On the table are a metal teapot, two damaged cups-and-saucers, and the remains of a breakfast—the latter consisting of a tin of condensed milk with a leaden spoon in it, a modicum of sugar in a screw of paper, and a cut loaf and a scrap of margarine. Also on the table, looking somewhat out of keeping with its surroundings, is a jug—minus its spout and handle—filled with pink and white roses.*

*At the nearer side of the window is a portable dwarf cupboard, and on the top of it are a penny bottle of ink, a pen-holder, two or three sheets of writing-paper and some envelopes, some crumpled picture-papers, and an empty beer-can.*

*On the floor by the arm-chair, unpolished and neglected, are Harmer's boots, on the left-hand side of the bed are his slippers, and against the wall between the coal-scuttle and the towel-horse is his hand-bag; and lying on the floor near the right-hand corner of the room there is a pair of woman's out-door shoes, down at heel and mud-stained.*

33

*Here and there the foul wall-paper is stripped from the walls, and the remnant of a hearthrug and a meagre square of greasy carpet do little to redeem the crusted dirt on the bare boards.*

*The left-hand side of the room is in shadow and only a dull light enters at the window; but a glint of sunshine strikes the farther side of the window-frame, giving a hint of a fine summer evening.*

[*Harmer and Lilian Dipple, in distorted attitudes, are lying on the bed asleep, he on the left-hand side of the bed with his face to the wall. From the court below rise the thin notes of a concertina on which a jig is being played. After a while there are two raps of the door-knocker. In time the knocking is repeated and then Lilian wakes and, raising herself on her elbow, stares stupidly at the door. She is wearing an old petticoat and a chemise of a dubious colour, and is a coarse-looking young woman with a tousled head and the smears of cheap paint on her cheeks.*

LILIAN. [*To herself, under her breath.*] 'Oo's that? [*Having studied the motionless figure beside her for a moment, she gets off the bed and—a little unsteadily— sticks her stockinged feet into her slippers. There is a third knocking.*] Oh, 'old yer noise! [*She goes to the door and opens it a few inches, the sound of the concertina ceasing as she peers through the aperture. Florence Portch is outside.*] Ullo, Flo!

FLORENCE. Kin I come in?

LILIAN. Yus. [*Opening the door far enough to admit Florence and no farther.*] Didn't know it was yew. [*As Florence enters.*] Don' maike a rah. My bloke's sleepin'.

FLORENCE. [*A puffy, overblown woman of five-and-forty, in dirty, dilapidated finery—her husky voice sinking to a whisper.*] Orl right.

LILIAN. [*Shutting the door softly.*] Sit dahn.

FLORENCE. [*Sitting in the chair at the farther side of the table.*] Bin on the booze ag'ine this mornin', both of yer, 'aven' yer?

LILIAN. [*Putting herself into her dressing-gown.*] Jest a bit.

FLORENCE. Thought I sore yer goin' the rahnd.

LILIAN. [*Approaching her.*] D'ye want h'enny-think?

FLORENCE. Depen's on wot theer is t'be 'ad, my deer.

LILIAN. Wotjer mean?

FLORENCE. Oh, don' s'y yer don' re-member! Lars night at the " Granby "!

LILIAN. [*Pinning up a straggling tail of hair.*] Lars night! I was fair gorn lars night. Wot 'appened?

FLORENCE. [*Jerking her thumb towards the man on the bed.*] 'E arst us—me an' some o' the boys—ter drop in 'ere this evenin' an' 'ave a free drink.

LILIAN. Did 'e? 'Ow many of yer?

FLORENCE. Theer was Perce, an' George, an' Alf Gorham—b'lieve that was th' lot.

LILIAN. [*Glancing at Harmer.*] Wonder if 'e rec'lec's.

FLORENCE. Gawd, I 'ope so. I tell yer I'm 'ard put to it 'ow ter git through these long bright evenin's.

LILIAN. [*Moving to the farther end of the table.*] They do 'ang 'eavy.

FLORENCE. *Yew* need'n' clack. In our biz'ness it's them that ain't as young as they was that's 'it by this stinkin' summer-time. [*Turning in her chair to watch Lilian, who is rearranging the roses in the jug.*] Lovelee fl'ar's yer got.

LILIAN. Lovelee.

FLORENCE. '*E* give 'em t'yer?

LILIAN. Bought 'em for me at the shop in Gr'ite Dover Street.

FLORENCE. Roses.

LILIAN. I chose roses. Might 'ave 'ad a big bunch o' 'andsome red things—gladoly—naime o' that sort. But No, I said. Roses f'r *me*, I said. Roses.

FLORENCE. [*Critically.*] Corst money.

LILIAN. [*Coming to the chair on the nearer side of the table.*] Not much chainge aht of a ten-shillin' note when *they* was paid for.

FLORENCE. Gen'leman, ain't 'e?

LILIAN. Thorer. [*She sits and the two women talk in undertones across the table.*] Aht an' aht.

FLORENCE. Wot's 'e doin' dahn ahr w'y, toff like 'im?

LILIAN. Oh, pleasher.

FLORENCE. Bin with yer neely a fortnight nah, 'as'n 'e?

LILIAN. Fortnight! Wotyer thinkin' of? Neely three weeks.

FLORENCE. Corse; fool I am. Sore yer tergether beginnin' o' the month.

LILIAN. [*With a touch of pride.*] Three weeks with *one*. My record.

FLORENCE. 'E's fond of ahr part o' the tahn, seemin'ly. 'E was rovin' abaht 'ere this time lars yeer, 'cordin' ter Alf an' George.

LILIAN. [*Indifferently.*] Oh?

FLORENCE. They see 'im a yeer ago in the Bridge Road, in the bar o' the " Lord Nelson."

LILIAN. [*In the same tone.*] Oh?

FLORENCE. An' they follered 'im ter the Distillery in the 'Igh Street.

LILIAN. [*Scowling.*] *Follered* 'im!

FLORENCE. An' then Alice Roberts took 'im in tow, an' they lors sight of 'im. Strainge they sh'd 'ave picked up with 'im ag'ine—George an' Alf—ain't it?

LILIAN. [*Between her teeth.*] Th'swine! I guess wot their gaime is. They'd strip the shirt orf 'im if I was'n' by. [*Fiercely.*] 'Ere! If I ketch 'em tryin' ter l'y 'ands on enny friend o' mine, I'll put th'p'leece on 'em; 's'truth I will! An' I'll push their blarsted faices in fust——!

    [*Her torrent of anger is checked by a rat-tat at the door.*

FLORENCE. 'Spect that's them.

LILIAN. [*Mutteringly.*] Curse 'em! [*Rising and going to the door.*] I wish they was dead an' rotten. [*She opens the door sharply and confronts a group of men on the landing.*] Nah, then!

CRICKMAY. [*A youth of the hooligan type, lean, pallid, close-cropped.*] Evenin'. Gen'leman in?

LILIAN. Oh, come in an' shut yer m'ar'th. [*Allowing Crickmay to pass her.*] 'E's 'avin a sleep.

KELK. [*A lank, loose-limbed, shambling young man in a dirty suit of shoddy—appearing in the doorway as Crickmay, after whistling a salutation to Florence, slouches to the fireplace.*] Evenin', Lil. [*Shaking hands with her.*] Fine evenin'. [*Entering.*] That ol' Flo?

LILIAN. [*Thrusting her elbow into his ribs as he passes her and pointing to Harmer.*] 'Ush, carn't yer! [*Greeting Gorham, who next appears—a bloated, pot-bellied person with a scrubby beard, older than his companions and dressed in greasy black.*] G'd evenin'.

GORHAM. [*With a leer which is meant to be ingratiating.*] G'd evenin', Miss Dipple. Gen'leman tol' us lars night ter look 'im up an' 'ave a talk with 'im abaht the des'prit staite o' the country—the scand'lous c'ndition o' the h'unemployed——

LILIAN. [*Again pointing to the bed as Gorham insinuates himself into the room.*] Well, yer kin see f'yerself 'e ain't taikin' enny des'prit staite o' the country jest at present. [*Closing the door.*] Sit dahn an' be quiet.

GORHAM. [*Moving to the trunk at the foot of the bed.*] G'd evenin', Miss Portch.

FLORENCE. Evenin'.

LILIAN. [*To Florence, pointing to the cupboard.*] Git aht the stuff, Flo, if yer kin find enny. [*As Florence goes to the cupboard—to Kelk, who is fingering the roses as if with the intention of selecting one for his button-hole.*] An' yew leave them fl'ar's be, George Kelk. [*Threateningly.*] If yer don't, Gaw' strike me stiff——!

KELK. Ow, not s'much lip!

[*They stand glowering at each other for a moment and then he sits astride the chair Florence has vacated.*

GORHAM. [*Seated on the trunk.*] We ain't 'ere, none of us, mealy f'r the saike o' the liquor. [*Lilian turns the chair on the right of the bed to face the visitors and sits in it sullenly*.] We're 'ere more f'r a p'litical discussion—f'r the puppose of exchaingin' views an' ideers——

LILIAN. [*To Gorham.*] Oh, keep it f'r Sunday! Y'ain't lecturin' t'a crard at the corner o' Lant Street ter-night, Alf Gorham. [*To Florence.*] That the on'y bottle, Flo?

[*Florence has taken from the cupboard a whisky-bottle about two-thirds full and has stood it upon the table. She now produces a couple of tumblers of the roughest kind and an earthenware mug; these she also puts on the table.*

FLORENCE. Theer's 'eaps o' bottles, but nothink in 'em.

LILIAN. [*Pointing to the empty beer-can on the top of the cupboard.*] Git some water, will yer? Me 'ead's swimmin' somethink awful. [*Motioning in the direction of the landing.*] Yer know w'ere the sink is, don-cher?

[*Florence picks up the can and is going to the door when she sees that Harmer has wakened and is sitting up.*

FLORENCE. Gen'leman's awaike! [*They all turn to Harmer, who is looking at everybody confusedly.*] G'd evenin'.

CRICKMAY. [*Who has installed himself in the arm-chair—as Lilian rises and goes to the right-hand side of the bed.*] Evenin', guvner.

KELK. Evenin'.

GORHAM. [*Rising and joining Lilian.*] G'd evenin' t'yer, mister.

LILIAN. [*To Harmer.*] 'Ow yer feelin' nah, deerie?

HARMER. Who—who——?

LILIAN. It's the boys — Alf Gorham—an' Perce Crickmay—an' George Kelk. An' theer's Flo—Flo Portch——

[*Harmer—his eyes bleared, his hair dank and dis-ordered, his face haggard and drawn—slips off the left-hand side of the bed and lurches forward. He is in his trousers and socks and a dingy shirt and collar, and his necktie is un-knotted.*

HARMER. [*Clutching at the bed-rail.*] What—what are they all doing here?

LILIAN. [*Coming to him.*] Yer arst 'em ter call in this evenin' an' 'ave a drink with us.

HARMER. [*Bemused.*] I—I asked them? *I* did?

CRICKMAY. Lars night at the "Granby." [*Pointing to Florence.*] I was interydooced t'yer by that lidy.

FLORENCE. That's right.

GORHAM. [*Advancing.*] An' we 'ad a argyment—Capital as agin Labour. H'england, I said——

KELK. [*Getting to his feet.*] Ow, if we ain't welcome——!

GORHAM. [*Oratorically.*] H'england, I said, form'ly feared an' respected, nah a ridic'lous byword in the kahnsels o' Europe——

HARMER. [*Clasping his temples.*] I—I forget—I—I forget——

CRICKMAY. [*Rising.*] Fergit!

LILIAN. [*To Crickmay.*] Yus, fergit. If yer don' 'ear pl'ine, go an' wash yer ears aht.

HARMER. [*To Lilian.*] Ssh, ssh, ssh! [*Shuddering.*] Is there any drink in the place?

LILIAN. Mor'n 'arf a bottle.

HARMER. Give it them; give it them, and let them take it away. [*Waving them all to the door.*] I—I'm sorry. I'm sorry.

CRICKMAY. Sorree! [*Joining Gorham and Florence at the table.*] 'Arf a bottle! It's h'us wot oughter be sorree.

[*There is a short, muttered dispute between Gorham, Florence, and Crickmay as to which of the three shall carry the bottle, Florence grabbing it from Gorham and Crickmay from Florence. Ultimately Gorham obtains possession of it and tucks it under his coat. While this is going on, Lilian goes to the door, to open it, and discovers Kelk in the act of run-*

*ning his hands over Harmer's overcoat, jacket,*
*and waistcoat.*

LILIAN. [*With a set jaw—opening the door and point-*
*ing to the landing.*] Git aht!

KELK. [*Disconcerted.*] Git aht!

LILIAN. Yus, git aht!

KELK. [*Blustering.*] L'k 'ere! 'Oo yer talkin' to in
that strine?

LILIAN. Ah, yer low scabby 'ound, yeh! If on'y I was
a man f'r a minute——!

KELK. Ow, go ter 'ell, yer common piece!

[*As he slinks away, Gorham, Crickmay, and Flor-*
*ence, casting disdainful glances at Harmer,*
*move to the door, which Lilian continues to*
*hold open.*

GORHAM. [*To Lilian.*] G'd evenin', Miss Dipple.

LILIAN. G'd evenin'.

CRICKMAY. [*To Lilian.*] S'long.

LILIAN. S'long.

FLORENCE. [*To Lilian, after the others have passed*
*out.*] See yer ag'ine laiter, p'r'aps?

LILIAN. Prob'ly.

[*Florence follows the men and Lilian closes the*
*door. Harmer has searched for his boots and*
*found them and, sitting in the arm-chair, has*
*pulled them on with feverish haste. He is now*
*trying, with trembling hands, to lace them.*
*Lilian shuffles across the room and, going*
*down on her knees, laces his boots for him.*

LILIAN. 'Ere! Lem'me——

HARMER. [*Recoiling.*] No, no; no, no——

LILIAN. G'arn! Tell yer I like w'itin' on yer.

HARMER. [*Leaning back to avoid contact with her and eyeing her with aversion.*] Th—thank you.

LILIAN. Yeh *'ave* 'ad a nice sleep, an' no error. Yeh bin layin' dahn f'r howers.

HARMER. [*Faintly.*] What time is it?

LILIAN. Gittin' on f'r 'ight, I sh'd s'y. Gim'me yer other foot.

HARMER. [*Obeying her.*] Thank you. [*After a pause.*] Lilian——

LILIAN. Yus?

HARMER. Do you—do you happen to know the date?

LILIAN. Daite?

HARMER. The day of the month. How far has the month gone?

LILIAN. Soon find aht f'r yer. [*Tying the second lace.*] Theer y'are.

HARMER. Thank you.

> [*She rises and goes to the cupboard and examines the picture-papers lying on the top of it. He watches her with increased horror and loathing.*

LILIAN. [*Reading the date on one of the papers.*] Toosd'y, twen'y-fust. That was yus'd'y. We ain't 'ad no piper ter-d'y.

HARMER. The twenty-second. [*Reckoning.*] Twenty-second—twenty-second—! [*Struggling out of the arm-chair and speaking more to himself than to her.*] I thought so! I dreamt it *must* be——!

LILIAN. [*Replacing the papers—carelessly.*] Well, wot abaht it?

> [*Turning up his shirt-cuffs, he staggers to the washhand-basin and pours some water into it from the toilet-jug. Then, rapidly, he washes his hands and splashes the water into his face.*

LILIAN. [*Approvingly.*] That's senserble; that'll put yer ter rights.

> [*She unhooks a skirt and a blouse from behind the curtain on the right of the door and brings them to the chair at the farther side of the table.*

LILIAN. [*Tossing the skirt and blouse on to the chair and unfastening her dressing-gown.*] Goin' aht ter git somethink ter eat nah, ain't we? [*He is drying his face and hands and doesn't answer her.*] H'y?

HARMER. [*Giving her an oblique look.*] N-n-no; not to-night, Lilian.

LILIAN. [*Staring at him.*] Wotjer mean, not ter-night?

HARMER. [*Arranging his necktie after a fashion.*] I—I can't stay with you any longer. My—my holiday's over.

> [*There is a short silence, during which he attempts to tidy his hair; then, in a matter-of-fact way, she dons her dressing-gown again. Readjusting his shirt-sleeves, he returns to her.*

LILIAN. [*Looking at him—simply.*] 'Ad 'nuf o' me?

HARMER. [*Avoiding her eye.*] N—no, it isn't that. It isn't that. I—[*Suddenly the playing of the concertina*

44

*starts afresh and, with a wild gesture, he breaks out frantically.*] Oh! Oh, that dreadful squeaking thing! That dreadful squeaking thing! [*Sinking on to the trunk at the foot of the bed and rocking himself to and fro.*] I shall never get rid of the sound of it. I shall always hear it. Oh, the dreadful, dreadful squeaking thing!

LILIAN. [*Mildly astonished at his outburst.*] Oh, don' be ser silly! Fancee bein' h'upset by a bleedin' concerteener! [*Fetching Harmer's jacket and waistcoat and handing the waistcoat to him.*] 'Ere——

HARMER. [*Taking the waistcoat from her and hurriedly putting it on.*] Thank you. [*Rising to put on his jacket, which she helps him into.*] Thank you. [*She brings him his overcoat and hat. He puts on his hat and she helps him into his overcoat.*] Thanks.

[*She picks up his bag and drags a soiled suit of pyjamas from beneath the patchwork coverlet. Cramming the pyjamas into the bag, she hunts for his slippers. These she also puts into the bag, and completes the packing by snatching the tooth-brush from the jam-pot and sticking it into one of the slippers. While she is thus occupied, Harmer, moving towards the table, takes a wallet from the breast-pocket of his jacket and empties it of its contents—a few pound-notes. Then he rummages in his trousers-pockets and finds another note, in a very crumpled state, and some silver and coppers. The playing of the concertina stops.*

LILIAN [*Giving him the bag.*] 'Ere——

45

HARMER. [*Taking the bag and presenting her with the money.*] This—this is all there is left.

LILIAN. [*Her eyes sparkling as she receives the money.*] H'orl! [*Stuffing the money into a pocket in her dressing-gown.*] If yer on'y knoo wot I git sometimes!

HARMER. I—I'll send you some more to-morrow, by post.

LILIAN. [*Nodding.*] Much erblige t'yer—w'ether yer mean it'r not.

HARMER. I do—I do mean it, I assure you. [*Holding out his hand.*] Good-bye.

LILIAN. [*Shaking his hand with great heartiness.*] Tat-tar. Taike care o' yerself. [*She lifts her face to his. He stiffens his body shrinkingly; at which, not comprehending, she raises her eyebrows.*] Ain't yer goin' ter?

HARMER. Er—of course. [*He forces himself to kiss her; then, wiping his lips furtively, he speaks in a blurred voice.*] F-f-forgive me.

LILIAN. [*Wonderingly.*] Fergive yer? Wot for?

[*He hesitates, then turns from her abruptly and goes to the door. There, bethinking himself, he halts and faces her again.*

HARMER. Oh—Lilian——

LILIAN. [*Who has followed him.*] Yus?

HARMER. Lend me those coppers, will you? I want to telephone to my—to my—I want to telephone. [*She takes the coins from her pocket and sorts out the pence.*] Tuppence will do.

LILIAN. [*Giving him two pennies.*] Don' yer wan' nothink f'r yer fare 'ome?

HARMER. [*Pocketing the pennies.*] No, thank you; I shall walk.

LILIAN. [*Surprised.*] Walk?

HARMER. [*Drawing a deep breath.*] Walk—walk—walk! Walk till it's almost daybreak! [*Opening the door.*] Good-bye once more.

LILIAN. Goo'-bye. Please ter see yer enny time yer this w'y.

HARMER. [*Passing out.*] Thank you.

LILIAN. [*Detaining him by seizing his coat.*] Deerie——!

HARMER. Eh?

LILIAN. If yer charnce ter come acrorst the boys ag'ine, mind yer give th' lousy brutes the go-by, woncher?

HARMER. [*Hurrying away.*] Yes—yes——

LILIAN. [*Going on to the landing and calling after him.*] Keep yer feet ahter them 'oles on the st'eers——!

[*The playing of the concertina is resumed as she comes back into the room. She closes the door and, sitting in the chair at the farther side of the table, begins to count her money. But her eyes falling on the flowers, she rises and fetches the toilet-jug and, quite impassively, proceeds to water them.*]

# THE FOURTH SCENE

*Outside Mrs. Nethercliff's house again. The light is the same as before.*

*[Harmer appears, coming along the gravel path. He is dressed as when last seen and is carrying his hand-bag. After glancing warily at the upper windows, he tiptoes to the door, puts his key in the lock, and lets himself in.*

# THE FIFTH SCENE

*Harmer's sitting-room at night-time. The room is cheerfully lighted and a fire is burning.*

*The date-box on the writing-table shows the date to be the fifteenth of May, and the flowers in the jardinières are the flowers of that month.*

*The disposition of the furniture is the same as at the beginning of the play.*

[*Propped up by a cushion, Harmer—the bright, attractive Harmer of the first scene—is lying on the settee, his feet to the door on the left, reading a book. His pipe is in his mouth and he is in his smoking-jacket and slippers. Presently Ida opens the door and enters.*

IDA. S'cuse me, sir——

HARMER. [*Lowering his book.*] Hallo!

IDA. Mr. Birkett, sir——

HARMER. [*Somewhat surprised.*] Mr. Birkett?

IDA. He apologises for calling so late, sir——

HARMER. [*Putting his feet to the ground.*] Calling on *me?*

IDA. Yessir, he particu'ly asked for you, sir; particu'ly.

HARMER. [*Rising.*] Bring Mr. Birkett in, Ida.

[*Ida disappears and Harmer, having knocked the ashes of his pipe into the grate, lays his book and pipe on the smoking-table. He is moving*

49

> towards the door to receive his visitor when
> Ida returns with Birkett.

IDA. [*Looking at Birkett admiringly as she announces him.*] Mr. Birkett.

HARMER. [*Shaking hands cordially with Birkett as Ida withdraws and closes the door.*] My dear fellow! A great pleasure!

> [*Birkett is a tall, stalwart young man of about two-and-thirty, dark-haired, and heavily moustached and wearing semi-clerical clothes. His face and lips are colourless and, though his voice is firm and rather strident, he has the manner of one who has come upon a distressful errand.*

BIRKETT. Thank you for seeing me at this hour, doctor.

HARMER. Delighted to see you at any hour. [*Eyeing him.*] You're cold. Have a warm. [*As Birkett goes to the fireplace—following him.*] Pretty nippy for the middle of May, isn't it?

BIRKETT. [*Holding his hands over the fire and then rubbing them.*] It is indeed. I've been walking up and down outside and I'm chilled to the bone.

HARMER. Walking up and down——?

BIRKETT. In the road, opposite.

HARMER. Why the devil didn't you—[*Laughingly.*] I beg your pardon—why didn't you come in? Elsie will be furious. We've only just shoo'd her off to bed.

BIRKETT. [*Turning to him.*] The fact is, Harmer, I've been waiting for her to retire—watching.

HARMER. Watching?

BIRKETT. Watching for the light in her room. I don't want to meet her to-night. I want a few words with you alone.

HARMER. [*Showing concern.*] My dear chap, aren't you well? Is this a professional visit?

BIRKETT. Oh, yes, I'm well—well physically, praise God. But mentally I am ill—sorely afflicted.

HARMER. I'm awfully grieved.

BIRKETT. [*With a wan smile.*] To-night, doctor, you must minister—what does our national poet say?— " minister to a mind diseased."

HARMER. [*Pointing to the settee and seating himself in the chair facing the fireplace.*] Sit down, old man. Tell me——

BIRKETT. [*Continuing to stand and gripping the lapels of his coat as if bracing himself for his task.*] Before I unburden myself to you, my good friend, let me give you my reason for approaching *you* in the matter which is weighing on me, instead of, in the first instance, speaking to the poor child upstairs and to that worthy woman, her aunt, Mrs. Nethercliff.

HARMER. [*Pricking up his ears.*] Speaking to Elsie and Mrs. Nethercliff——?

BIRKETT. You are the male of this household. Owing to qualities which nobody appreciates more fully than I do, you have wound yourself round the hearts of Mrs. Nethercliff and Miss Speed until the aunt has come to regard you as a son and the niece to look upon you as a brother. I esteem you as the head of this little family.

HARMER. [*Uneasily.*] I'm afraid that's putting it a bit too high, Birkett.

BIRKETT. I believe not; truly I believe not. At any rate, I am sure you have considerable influence with these ladies; and I am equally sure that you are a person capable of dealing in the spirit of Christian charity with a fellow-creature whose flesh—in the language of the Bible—is torn with the thorns of the wilderness and with briers.

HARMER. [*Now thoroughly apprehensive of the nature of Birkett's business—leaning back in his chair and speaking almost curtly.*] What's amiss, Birkett? [*After a pause, during which Birkett's chin sinks on to his breast.*] Eh?

> [*With an effort, Birkett pulls himself together, squares his shoulders, and sits resolutely on the settee.*

BIRKETT. Harmer, my relations with Miss Speed, as they are at present, have got to cease. Our conditional engagement must be put an end to—the tie must be severed.

HARMER. [*Dryly.*] Ah? [*Examining his nails.*] H'm! I thought that was coming.

BIRKETT. Of course, it's most irregular of me to spring this announcement on you in such an informal fashion. I—I meant to state my case in writing——

HARMER. Quite so; quite so.

BIRKETT. [*Nursing his head wearily.*] But I'm not sleeping—I haven't slept for several nights—and a sudden impulse seized me about half-an-hour ago——

HARMER. [*Jumping up.*] Confound it! I suppose you don't care a twopenny damn whether *I* sleep or not!

BIRKETT. [*Protesting.*] Oh, my dear sir——!

HARMER. [*Pacing the room.*] What's at the bottom of this, Birkett? Are those precious scruples of yours still giving you the gripes?

BIRKETT. [*Stiffening himself.*] Please don't insult me, Harmer.

HARMER. Oh, you must forgive me for saying that I don't propose to study your feelings in this affair in the least. I'm thinking of Elsie—only of Elsie—my sister, if you choose to call her that. [*Halting at the left of the round table and rapping the table imperatively.*] Come, Birkett! Out with it! The girl's health is no worse than when you fell in love with her last year, and encouraged her to fall in love with you; rather better, I fancy. What's happened to make you sound the retreat all in a hurry? Anything—or nothing?

BIRKETT. [*Rising and advancing to the right of the round table and confronting Harmer.*] I regret the tone you see fit to adopt towards me, Harmer; but I'll answer your inquiries. [*Drawing himself up.*] Yes, my scruples *are* still troubling me, and more acutely than ever. Beyond that, nothing has occurred to cause me to decide—as, with the aid of prayer, I have at length decided—that my position is one from which my sacred obligations demand that I shall extricate myself. I do love Miss Speed——

HARMER. [*Turning away and throwing himself into the chair at the writing-table.*] T'sha——!

53

BIRKETT. I do love Miss Speed. But, with every respect for your contrary opinion, the conviction has forced itself upon me that she will never be blest with perfect health. Reflect! Can't you understand—won't you try to understand—the difficulty I have placed myself in? Constant anxiety for an ailing wife, and the unremitting attention she would have the right to expect from me, would be fatal to my appointed career. I repeat, I do love Miss Speed; but I love my people also—the sheep of my shepherding—and, with a clearness of vision withheld from me at the moment of my infatuation, I recognize that their claim upon me is paramount, supreme. [*Sitting in the chair at the farther side of the round table and thumping the table with his clenched hands.*] My people! My people! I sacrifice myself to my people, Harmer.

HARMER. [*Scornfully.*] Ha! Poor little Elsie has become one of your flock. *She* bruises her knees worshipping in your sheep-pen. You are sacrificing her, too, it appears!

BIRKETT. [*Feebly.*] She entered into the arrangement willingly, Harmer; I implore you to remember that. She was a consenting party.

HARMER. Consenting party! As much as Miss Lamb is a consenting party when she's gobbled up by Mister Wolf.

BIRKETT. [*Writhing.*] Harmer! Harmer! This is cowardly of you.

HARMER. [*Springing up and standing over Birkett.*] Cowardly! You're a nice fellow to talk of cowardice!

54

Why do you come to me in your scrape? Because I'm the captain of the ship, you say. That's a lie; a lying pretence.

BIRKETT. [*Looking up at him with flashing eyes.*] Harmer! Be careful! How dare you!

HARMER. Oh, you mayn't know you're lying, Birkett; I'll allow that. But you are, none the less. You come to me because you haven't the nerve to break the news to the women themselves. [*Crossing to the fireplace determinedly.*] Well, I decline to take the job on; [*pressing the bell-push, which is on the left-hand side of the mantelpiece*] I'm not going to pull your chestnuts out of the fire for you. [*Glancing at a clock on the mantelpiece.*] Mrs. Nethercliff won't have gone to bed yet. [*Facing Birkett.*] Sorry, Birkett, to make myself so unpleasant.

BIRKETT. [*Rising, deadly calm.*] And I am sorry, Harmer, to find you a different sort of man from the man I've always taken you to be. [*Moving a step or two towards Harmer.*] You will repent this treatment of me. [*Losing his self-restraint and extending his arms passionately.*] I cry aloud out of the depth of my sufferings and I warn you that you will repent this treatment of me——

HARMER. [*Hearing a sound in the passage.*] Sssh——!
[*Birkett drops his arms and steadies himself as the door opens and Ida reappears.*

IDA. [*To Harmer.*] D'you ring, sir?

HARMER. Mrs. Nethercliff hasn't gone upstairs yet, has she, Ida?

IDA. No, sir; not yet.

HARMER. Tell her that Mr. Birkett and I would like to see her, if she can spare us a few minutes.

IDA. [*Vanishing.*] Yessir.

> [*Birkett waits for Ida to close the door, and then, with his hands clasped behind him, walks about in a ferment. Strolling to the smoking-table, Harmer picks up a box of cigarettes.*

HARMER. [*Proffering the box.*] You don't smoke?

BIRKETT. [*Shaking his head.*] No.

> [*Harmer is lighting a cigarette and Birkett is in the middle of the room, in front of the round table, when the door is opened again and Mrs. Nethercliff enters with a cheerful air. She is trimly dressed in an evening gown of black taffeta.*

MRS. NETHERCLIFF. [*Shutting the door.*] How do you do, Mr. Birkett? [*Going to Birkett and shaking his limp and unresponsive hand.*] Very naughty of you to call as late as this. Elsie will be dreadfully vexed— [*observing something in his expression which startles her, and drawing back*] eh? [*Staring first at Birkett and then at Harmer, who has returned to the fireplace and is frowning into the fire.*] Is—is anything wrong? What—what is it?

BIRKETT. [*Sullenly.*] Dr. Harmer has taken it upon himself to send for you, Mrs. Nethercliff. [*Leaving her and resuming his walk.*] I won't deprive him of the agreeable task of explaining why.

[*Her eyes follow Birkett for a few seconds, then she goes to Harmer and touches his sleeve.*

MRS. NETHERCLIFF. [*Falteringly.*] Is it anything concerning—Elsie?

HARMER. [*Turning to her.*] Yes.

MRS. NETHERCLIFF. [*Under her breath.*] Oh——!

HARMER. [*Gently.*] You guess——?

MRS. NETHERCLIFF. [*Nodding.*] Yes—[*sitting undemonstratively in the chair facing the fireplace*] I guess. [*In a whisper.*] Poor little soul!

HARMER. Mr. Birkett, after much heart-searching, has come to the conclusion that the engagement, or whatever you term it, between him and Elsie must be quashed. He's convinced she'll never be robust, and that his marrying her would be ruinous to the chief purpose of his life—his spiritual labours. [*Tossing the remains of his cigarette into the fire—grimly.*] How's that, Birkett?

BIRKETT. [*Coming forward.*] Thank you, Harmer. You put it bluntly, but with fairness. [*Inclining his head.*] I thank you.

MRS. NETHERCLIFF. [*Producing her handkerchief and wiping away a tear.*] This is a shock, of course; but I'm not altogether surprised. I've noticed that Mr. Birkett has been dropping away from us recently. [*Beating her hands together softly.*] Oh, but it's cruel, cruel, cruel!

BIRKETT. [*Addressing the back of Mrs. Nethercliff's chair—hotly.*] To Miss Speed, perhaps; but hardly to you, Mrs. Nethercliff. It would be affectation on your part to profess that this is a blow to you personally. [*Again walking about the room.*] You have never liked me; never. I admit that you have striven against your prejudices, but the prospect of my marrying your niece has always been distasteful to you. [*Flourishing his arms.*] Well, now you can rejoice—rejoice—congratulate yourself that you are rid of me—rid of me——

> [*A playful tattoo on the door on the left pulls him up sharply behind the round table. They all look towards the door and, after a short silence, the drumming is repeated.*

MRS. NETHERCLIFF. [*Rising and calling out in a frightened voice.*] Who's that?

> [*The door opens and Elsie pokes her head into the room roguishly.*

ELSIE. Ah! Ha, ha, ha, ha——!

MRS. NETHERCLIFF. [*Aghast.*] Elsie!

> [*Elsie enters—a charming vision in spite of her fragile appearance. Her feet are in " mules " and her hair is gathered into a loose knot, and she is clad in a pink " Princess " petticoat and a white dressing-jacket edged with swansdown.*

ELSIE. [*Having closed the door—to everybody.*] Don't be scandalized; I'm quite decent. [*Advancing to Birkett.*] Ida's just told me you're here. [*Holding out her hands to him.*] What a stranger you are, Oswald!

BIRKETT. [*Recoiling.*] Don't—don't—! [*Wildly.*] They'll tell you—they'll tell you——

[*He brushes past her and goes out, pulling the door
to after him. She stands for a moment dum-
founded; then she runs to the door and
opens it. As she does so, the front-door slams.
Again there is a silence, during which Elsie
gazes blankly into the passage and Mrs.
Nethercliff moves to the front of the round
table.*]

MRS. NETHERCLIFF. [*Stretching out her arms to the
girl.*] Elsie——!

ELSIE. [*Shutting the door and going to Mrs. Nethercliff.*] What—what have I done? What have I done,
aunt?

MRS. NETHERCLIFF. [*Clasping Elsie to her.*] Oh, my
dear, my dear, my dear!

ELSIE. [*Releasing herself and backing away from
Mrs. Nethercliff fearfully.*] Well? He said you'd tell
me. Go on. Tell me.

MRS. NETHERCLIFF. To-morrow—in the morning—

ELSIE. No, no; to-night—at once. [*Stamping her
foot.*] Tell me. [*Mrs. Nethercliff glances helplessly
at Harmer, whereupon Elsie runs to him and grips
his shoulders.*] Walter! [*Tightening her grip.*]
Walter—!

HARMER. [*Removing her hands and fondling them.*]
Sssh, sssh, sssh! Try not to be upset, old lady. Take
my advice; don't waste another thought on the fellow.
[*She slowly withdraws her hands from his.*] Let him
marry some cast-iron female with a bald forehead and
prominent teeth. That's *his* mark.

ELSIE. He—he—he has cried off, do you mean? [*Receiving only a compassionate shrug in reply, she turns to Mrs. Nethercliff.*] He—he has thrown me over?

MRS. NETHERCLIFF. Mr. Birkett is still afraid, Elsie —still afraid——

ELSIE. Afraid——?

MRS. NETHERCLIFF. He's still afraid that, if you were his wife, his anxiety on your account would—would——

HARMER. Would make him neglect his blessed sheep.

MRS. NETHERCLIFF. And so—and so he thinks it wiser in the circumstances——

ELSIE. But—but—but he's not giving me a proper chance! I'm growing stronger every month. [*To Mrs. Nethercliff, fiercely.*] You know I am! [*To Harmer.*] You know I am!

HARMER. [*Soothingly.*] Elsie, Elsie, Elsie——!

ELSIE. You—you know I am. You——

[*She staggers and falls against Harmer and he partly leads, partly carries, her to the settee and lays her upon it, her head to the door on the left. Then he goes quickly into his consulting room, while Mrs. Nethercliff hurries to Elsie and kneels beside her.*

MRS. NETHERCLIFF. Darling—darling——!

ELSIE. [*Moaning into a cushion.*] Oh! Oh! Oh!

MRS. NETHERCLIFF. No, no; no, no! Don't take it in this way, Elsie; don't take it in this way!

ELSIE. Oh! Oh——!

MRS. NETHERCLIFF. It has been a mistake from the

beginning. Thank heaven you're free from the wretched entanglement.

ELSIE. Oh——!

MRS. NETHERCLIFF. There, there, there! To-morrow you'll see things clearer; the daylight will put another aspect on things. That fool Ida, to be such a busy-body! I could slap her stupid face. [*With extreme tenderness, stroking Elsie's hair.*] My pet, my lambkin, my treasure——!

ELSIE. [*Shrinking under Mrs. Nethercliff's caresses.*] Oh, please leave me alone! Please, please leave me alone!

> [*Harmer returns, carrying a conical measure containing a small dose of a colourless liquid. Standing behind the settee, he hands the glass to Mrs. Nethercliff.*]

HARMER. [*To Elsie, lifting her up.*] Here you are, little 'un! Swallow that. [*Elsie takes the glass from Mrs. Nethercliff and drinks the contents.*] Clicquot, extra dry! [*Placing the empty glass on the smoking-table.*] Brava!

> [*Slowly the girl puts her feet to the ground and, after passing her hand across her brow, looks fixedly at Mrs. Nethercliff.*]

ELSIE. [*In a low, tremulous, but biting tone.*] Yes, this is big triumph for you, aunt, isn't it? A glorious victory!

MRS. NETHERCLIFF. [*Faintly.*] Elsie!

ELSIE. You always hated him; always loathed the idea of our marriage. How you must be exulting—

[*hitting her breast*] exulting inside you! Chortling!

HARMER. [*As Mrs. Nethercliff rises in perturbation.*]
Shut up, Elsie! Shame!

ELSIE. [*To Mrs. Nethercliff, gathering force as she
proceeds.*] You don't care really—not a row of pins—
what humiliation, what disgrace, I suffer through
Oswald's backing out. [*Getting off the settee shakily
and confronting Mrs. Nethercliff with flaming eyes.*]
All you care for is that I should give up chapel and
attend St. Barnabas's again; that's all you care for,
aunt.

MRS. NETHERCLIFF. [*Piteously.*] Oh, Elsie——!

ELSIE. [*Withdrawing from Mrs. Nethercliff's reach.*]
Don't touch me! [*Supporting herself by clutching the
chair facing the fireplace.*] Don't touch me!

HARMER. [*To Mrs. Nethercliff.*] Phsst——!

[*With a significant gesture he motions Mrs.
Nethercliff to the other side of the room and
she moves away to the writing-table.*

MRS. NETHERCLIFF. [*Wringing her hands.*] Oh, my
child! My child!

HARMER. [*To Elsie.*] Look here, young woman, if
you don't calm yourself and sit down, you'll topple over
and break that pretty nose of yours; in which event *I*
won't mend it. [*Turning to the round table as she sinks
into the chair.*] And what the blazes do you mean by
howling about humiliation and disgrace? Who is humili-
ated, who's disgraced? Not you.

MRS. NETHERCLIFF. [*Now seated at the writing-table,
crying quietly into her handkerchief.*] Very few people

know of the affair between you and Mr. Birkett, Elsie;
very few.

HARMER. [*Sitting at the round table.*] And even if it
were known generally——

ELSIE. [*Shaking her fists in the air.*] Of course it's
known generally. Half Streatham knows it. Do you
imagine the friends we've confided in haven't spread it
all over the place? Why, people who are almost total
strangers to me have made sly allusions to it! [*Forgetting Harmer's injunction and struggling out of her
chair.*] Oh, I shall never hold up my head again; I shall
never hold up my head again!

HARMER. [*Pointing to the settee.*] Elsie——!

ELSIE. [*Sitting on the settee, the light of a sudden
resolve in her eyes.*] Oh, yes, I will, though! [*Breathlessly.*] I'll have my revenge on Oswald Birkett. I'll
show him how little I mind his chucking me. If he
won't marry me, some other man will. I swear to God
I'll be married before the year's out!

MRS. NETHERCLIFF. [*Horrified.*] Elsie——!

ELSIE. [*Not heeding the interruption—her words
pouring from her in a torrent.*] Clive Morgan—Clive
Morgan—he's been desperately gone on me for ages. A
word of encouragement and I've got Clive right enough.
His sister Stella—my great pal—Stella would fix that
up. The old Morgans, too—they doat on me! And
Teddy Kentish, the boy who saved me from being
knocked down by the motor-lorry outside Hemming
and Smart's, the drapers; his prospects are better than
Clive's. Teddy was cracked about me once. My being

white and skinny didn't matter a bean to Teddy Kent-ish. It's only Mr. Birkett who funks seeing a medicine-bottle in the house occasionally. Oh, but I'll teach the Reverend Oswald Birkett! I'll mortify him; I'll wound him as deeply as he's wounded me. [*Lying at full length on the settee again, her head to the fireplace and her face buried in a cushion.*] The brute, to make me love him! The brute, to make me love him! [*Her voice dying away.*] Brute—brute—brute——!

> [*Mrs. Nethercliff has risen and crept to Harmer, who, with an eager expression, is staring into space.*

MRS. NETHERCLIFF. [*In his ear.*] What shall I do? What shall I do? Advise me; advise me. [*He doesn't stir.*] Walter——!

HARMER. [*Starting.*] Eh?

MRS. NETHERCLIFF. Shall we get her to bed now, and talk to her in the morning? [*Finding he is still self-absorbed.*] Oh, help me; help me!

HARMER. [*Rousing himself.*] Yes—yes—[*With the air of a man who has come to a decision, he goes to the door on the left and opens it. Holding the door-handle, he beckons to Mrs. Nethercliff and, puzzled by his manner, she joins him.*] I—I've something to say to Elsie—er—privately. I won't keep her long. [*She nods and passes him and, with a wondering look, departs. His head in the passage, he watches her till she is out of sight; then he shuts the door and advances to Elsie.*] Elsie—[*She sobs.*] Elsie dear——

ELSIE [*In a muffled voice.*] What do you want?

HARMER. Your aunt's left us; we're by ourselves. [*Drawing the chair which is opposite to the fireplace to a position closer to the settee.*] Listen. [*Sitting.*] Can you hear me? [*She utters an inarticulate sound in assent.*] Elsie—what do you say to paying Birkett out by—by marrying *me*?

ELSIE. [*After a pause, raising her head slightly.*] You!

HARMER. You needn't give me an answer to-night—nor to-morrow—nor next week. Take your time.

ELSIE. [*Lifting herself with a jerk into a sitting posture and facing him with wild eyes.*] Walter!

HARMER. [*Smiling at her wistfully.*] Well?

ELSIE. But you're my brother! At least, I—I think of you as my brother.

HARMER. You could soon cure yourself of *that*, if you had the will to. [*By degrees she puts her feet to the ground, arranging her petticoat about her ankles circumspectly.*] Without pledging yourself—how does my suggestion strike you?

ELSIE. You—you've completely taken my breath away. [*Plucking at the trimming of her jacket.*] I'd no idea you—you had this sort of liking for me.

HARMER. Nor had *I*—consciously—till a minute ago.

ELSIE. A minute ago?

HARMER. When you threatened to get even with Birkett by chasing the eligible youths of the district.

ELSIE. I meant it! I meant it! I meant it!

HARMER. [*His fingers tightly interlocked.*] And then—suddenly—as if a streak of lightning had stabbed my brain—the notion flashed through me that it might be possible to give our affection for each other another shape. [*Bending forward.*] I'd be jolly good to you, Elsie; whether you were lusty or weakly, I'd be jolly good to you.

> [*Again there is a pause, during which she shifts in her seat waveringly. Then she deliberately holds out her hand to him.*

ELSIE. Right you are! I'm game.

HARMER. [*Transferring himself from the arm-chair to the settee and taking her hand.*] Ah——!

ELSIE. [*Her bosom heaving.*] So much for Oswald Birkett! So much for Oswald Birkett! When—when shall we be married, Walter?

HARMER. [*Feverishly.*] The end of July—the thirty-first of July——

ELSIE. [*With increasing excitement.*] The day before your summer holiday begins?

HARMER. [*Crumpling her hand and nodding.*] Yes —yes——

ELSIE. Your holiday will be our honeymoon?

HARMER. Yes.

ELSIE. Where shall we go? Shall we go abroad?

HARMER. Certainly, if you wish to.

ELSIE. Irene Burgess and her husband went to Etretat last August. They rave about it.

HARMER. Do they?

ELSIE. Or there's Switzerland! Would Switzerland agree with me?

HARMER. At a moderate height.

ELSIE. [*Tidying her hair, which has become straggled, and laughing mechanically.*] Ha, ha! It'll be a very different holiday from the holidays you've been spending ever since you've lived with aunt and me, won't it?

HARMER. [*Sitting erect and speaking in a pleasant but artificial voice.*] Very—very.

ELSIE. [*Her tone changing to one of curiosity.*] Walter——

HARMER. Eh?

ELSIE. Those funny holidays of yours; auntie has fretted herself blue over them! [*Edging nearer to him.*] Shall I tell you what she has got into her head with regard to your holidays?

HARMER. [*As before.*] What she's—got into her head——?

ELSIE. She believes that, instead of hiding yourself in a quiet nook in the country, as you've led us to suppose, you've sneaked off to some nasty, poverty-stricken part of London; which would account for your always coming back to us looking so horribly seedy and fagged out.

HARMER. [*Loosening his shirt-collar.*] Oh—auntie believes that, does she?

ELSIE. [*Slyly.*] Is it a true bill? [*His collar still troubles him.*] Walter——

HARMER. Well, I—I confess auntie isn't altogether on the wrong tack.

[*He rises and walks away to the round table and traces a pattern on it with his finger.*

67

ELSIE. Oh, Walter, as if you weren't sufficiently kind to the poor here, for eleven months out of the twelve. I've no patience with you, playing such silly antics!

HARMER. [*His back to her.*] Anyhow, I play them no more. No more! [*She rises and goes to him.*] Thank God, this clinches it; [*between his teeth*] this—this clinches it! [*Hearing the rustle of her petticoat, he turns to her and catches her two hands and crushes them against his breast.*] Oh, thank God, Elsie! Thank God, Elsie! Thank God——!

ELSIE. [*Wincing.*] Sss! You're hurting me——

[*He releases her and goes to the writing-table and alters the date in the date-box.*

HARMER. [*As he does so—quiveringly.*] To-morrow! Wake up to a new life to-morrow, Elsie! New life! New life——!

ELSIE. [*Sitting at the round table, and astonished at the oddity of his behaviour.*] Walter—[*He replaces the date-box and collects himself.*] What's the matter with you? Why will our getting married—clinch something? What will it—clinch? [*Peevishly.*] What does—clinch signify exactly?

HARMER. [*At her side, but so that the play of his features is concealed from her—lightly.*] In the present case, old lady, it signifies that the little understanding we've just arrived at confirms a resolution to relinquish a bad habit.

ELSIE. [*Glancing up at him.*] Sacrificing your rest as you've been doing?

68

HARMER. That's it; sacrificing my rest as I've been doing.

ELSIE. [*Quizzingly.*] And you're sure there's no—danger——?

HARMER. Danger——?

ELSIE. Of your neglecting me by-and-by?

HARMER. Neglecting you?

ELSIE. Indulging yourself again in your fancy for—what's the name of it?—humani—humanitarianism?

HARMER. Ho, ho! That's a big word for your small mouth!

ELSIE. [*Her brow darkening.*] It's one of Oswald's; [*curling her lip*] I've heard *him* use it.

HARMER. [*Grasping her shoulder.*] No, there's no danger; not the remotest.

ELSIE. [*Pouting.*] You may have formed similar resolutions before, for all I know, and broken them.

HARMER. [*His face contracting in pain.*] Yes; but this—this——

ELSIE. This—clinches it?

HARMER. This clinches it. [*Bending over her.*] And now run away to your aunt and tell her that you're actually engaged—ha, ha, ha!—engaged to the handsomest young man for miles round. [*Assisting her to rise.*] I'll join you both in five minutes.

> [*Followed by Elsie, he goes to the door on the left and opens it; and then they stand facing each other, he hesitatingly, she shyly. After a moment or two he advances his lips to hers, but she covers her mouth with the back of her*

69

*hand and offers him her forehead. He kisses her, and she passes him and disappears into the passage; whereupon he closes the door and roves about the room elatedly.*

HARMER. [*To himself.*] Ah! Ah! Ah! Thank God! Thank God! Thank God!

[*His walk brings him to the settee, on which he sits with clasped hands; but he has scarcely seated himself when, repressing a shout, he sinks to the floor and kneels at the settee in an attitude of passionate thanksgiving.*

# THE SIXTH SCENE

*Harmer's sitting-room once more, the light being the
same as when the room was first seen.*

*The date in the date-box is now the twenty-fifth
of June and again the grate is fireless, and again
the flowers in the jardinières are the flowers of full
summer.*

*The arrangement of the furniture is still as it
was at the opening of the play.*

[*There is nobody in the room, but presently Ida
enters at the door on the left followed by Mac-
Gill. Ida is glowing with pleasure.*

IDA. It *is* nice to see you again, sir. Been away,
haven't you?

MACGILL. I have, Ida.

IDA. [*Motioning to the consulting-room.*] Dr. Harmer's got a patient with him. I'll take your name in.

MACGILL. No, no; don't bother him till he's disen-
gaged. [*Passing her.*] Are the ladies at home?

IDA. Yessir.

MACGILL. [*Strolling to the fireplace.*] You might let
'em know I'm here, will you?

IDA. Yessir.

MACGILL. [*Turning to her.*] Very excited about the
wedding next month, Ida?

IDA. [*At the door.*] Oh, frightfully, sir; more'n I can
say.

MACGILL. Ha, ha, ha! A great event!

IDA. [*Half in the passage.*] Hope you're coming to us, like you did last year, sir, while Dr. Harmer and Miss Elsie are on their honeymoon.

MACGILL. There is a strong probability, Ida, that your pious hope will be fulfilled. In fact——

IDA. Here *is* Mrs. Nethercliff, sir——

[*Mrs. Nethercliff, in a flutter, brushes past Ida and goes to MacGill with extended hands.*

MRS. NETHERCLIFF. [*To MacGill.*] I thought I heard your voice! [*To Ida.*] Tell Miss Elsie, Ida.

IDA. [*Withdrawing and closing the door.*] Yes'm.

MRS. NETHERCLIFF. [*Her hands in MacGill's.*] How are you?

MACGILL. As well as an old chap can be who has been spending six weeks with an aged and querulous sister in that stuffy hole the Isle of Wight.

MRS. NETHERCLIFF. When did you get back?

MACGILL. Yesterday.

MRS. NETHERCLIFF. [*With a smile of gratification.*] And this afternoon——!

MACGILL. Don't flatter yourself, madam; my call isn't on *you*. I've run over to ask Harmer whether I can be of help to him again in August.

MRS. NETHERCLIFF. Bless you! He was going to beg you to repeat your kindness. [*Pointing to the settee.*] Sit down. [*Seating herself in the chair fronting the fireplace—eagerly.*] What do you think of it all?

MACGILL. [*Continuing to stand.*] Think of it——?

MRS. NETHERCLIFF. The news you had from me at

Bembridge—Elsie and Walter! Man alive, I wrote you three of four sheets!

MACGILL. Didn't you get my answer?

MRS. NETHERCLIFF. A scrappy answer. Congratulations! What are congratulations?

MACGILL. Everything, if they're sincere.

MRS. NETHERCLIFF. You're really pleased?

MACGILL. Honestly pleased. It's splendid.

MRS. NETHERCLIFF. Oh, my dear friend! It does me good to hear you say so. [*A note of anxiety in her face.*] I ought to be extremely happy.

MACGILL. [*Raising his eyebrows.*] *Aren't* you?

MRS. NETHERCLIFF. I—I suppose I am.

MACGILL. Why, what's troubling you?

MRS. NETHERCLIFF. Elsie—a little.

MACGILL. Elsie?

MRS. NETHERCLIFF. I wish *she* was happier.

MACGILL. In better health, do you mean?

MRS. NETHERCLIFF. Her health is fairly satisfactory. I mean I wish I could see her looking in better spirits —less moody, less inclined to mope and sit with her hands in her lap, staring at the pattern on the wallpaper. She isn't enormously interested in the preparations for her trousseau! It pains me to watch her.

MACGILL. P'sh! [*Sitting on the settee.*] She'll be easier in her mind when she's married. She's had a bit of a shock, remember—the scurvy way she was treated by the other fellow—Mr.—Mr.——

MRS. NETHERCLIFF. Birkett.

MACGILL. When a young girl makes a small god of a man and he lets her down, she loses faith in the stability of the universe. The earth rocks under her feet, and the human race—the male part of it—seems nothing but vermin on the crawl.

MRS. NETHERCLIFF. But now there's Walter!

MACGILL. There *will* be Walter. They're not husband and wife yet. Against her reason, she may even doubt *his* sincerity.

MRS. NETHERCLIFF. Nobody could doubt Walter.

MACGILL. Besides, why expect her to be skipping about as if she were a gazelle—do gazelles skip?—as if she were a chamois? She's a modest lass, for these days; as she nears the brink, she may feel a trifle scared.

MRS. NETHERCLIFF. [*Rising and pacing the room restlessly.*] You'll see her in a minute. She's dressing to go out. At least, she has promised to go out.

MACGILL. [*Puzzled.*] Promised——?

MRS. NETHERCLIFF. Except for a stroll in the garden, she hasn't left the house more than a dozen times since Mr. Birkett finally relieved us of his saintly presence. And fresh air and exercise are absolutely necessary for her!

MACGILL. Harmer's fault. He should insist on her going out.

MRS. NETHERCLIFF. He does his best, but he always ends by humouring her. You can't be doctor *and* lover. She used to be so fond of being out of doors! I can't understand it. She's as obstinate as the Pekingese puppy he's just given her. It's incomprehensible, her stubbornness!

MACGILL. [*Thoughtfully.*] H'm! [*Rubbing his head.*] Is Mr. Birkett still in the neighbourhood?

MRS. NETHERCLIFF. Of course. His chapel hasn't been considerate enough to remove itself. [*Halting at the round table.*] You think she's afraid of coming face to face with him on her walks?

MACGILL. Not unnatural, if she is.

MRS. NETHERCLIFF. But when we propose to accompany her—either of us—she resents it; is quite angry. The other day——[*listening*] ssh! [*The door on the left opens and Elsie appears, charmingly dressed for the street and with a Pekingese dog in her arms. Her manner is languid and fretful, and her eyes have a strained, abstracted look.*] Elsie darling, here's Dr. MacGill!

MACGILL. [*Rising.*] Ha, ha! All that remains of him after his travels.

ELSIE. [*Shutting the door and advancing to MacGill, who meets her in the middle of the room—chillingly.*] Why, you've only been to the Isle of Wight, Dr. Mac-Gill.

MACGILL. [*Putting her hand to his lips in gallant fashion.*] Ho, what a precise little person! The Isle of Wight is the farthest corner of the globe when you're separated from the adored one.

ELSIE. [*With a thin smile.*] Am I the adored one?

MACGILL. [*Romantically.*] Whom else in all the world!

MRS. NETHERCLIFF. [*Standing behind the writing-table.*] Now, doctor, be careful, or I'll tear your eyes out!

MACGILL. [*Blowing a kiss to Mrs. Nethercliff.*] Ha, ha, ha, ha! [*Pinching the dog's ear.*] I say, that's a handsome beast! I envy him. There's nobody to clasp me to her buzzom and pet and spoil me.

ELSIE. A present from Walter. [*Regarding the dog with disfavour.*] He's a dreadful nuisance. I never wanted this sort of animal.

MRS. NETHERCLIFF. Elsie——!

ELSIE. [*Peevishly.*] I didn't, aunt; you know I didn't. Horrid little loiterer!

MRS. NETHERCLIFF. Most ungracious of you, Elsie. Such a perfectly bred dog!

ELSIE. He isn't. His legs are too long, Stella Morgan says, and his coat's a great deal too short.

MRS. NETHERCLIFF. [*Indignantly.*] Stella Morgan——!

MACGILL. [*Interposing in a hurry and laying his hands on Elsie's shoulders.*] At any rate I must be sure that *my* coat is the correct cut—the coat I wear at a wedding which is to take place shortly. I intend to be a terrific swell on that occasion.

ELSIE. [*Releasing herself.*] Thank you; thank you, Dr. MacGill, but I—I'm sick to death of being spoken to about it.

MRS. NETHERCLIFF. Elsie——!

ELSIE. [*Suddenly on the verge of tears.*] Oh, stop worrying me. If only people wouldn't worry me——!

[*Harmer enters from the consulting-room, his appearance more youthful, his bearing more buoyant, than ever.*

HARMER. My dear MacGill! [*Closing the leaf of the folding-doors.*] I've been pitching into Ida for not telling me you were here. [*Coming between MacGill and Elsie and shaking hands with MacGill vigorously.*] An elderly gentleman with nothing the matter with him has been boring me stiff.

MACGILL. Ha, ha! Here's another on the same errand.

HARMER. [*To Elsie.*] Hallo, old lady! Going out? By Jove, there's no keeping you indoors! [*Stroking her chin.*] You went for a walk less than a week ago! You *are* a gadling!

ELSIE. [*Jerking her head aside.*] Oh, don't tease me, Walter! Don't tease me!

HARMER. Sorry, sweetheart. [*Patting the dog.*] Where are you and Mr. Wu off to?

ELSIE. To—to—to Stella Morgan's to tea perhaps. She—she—[*turning away abruptly*] good-bye, Dr. MacGill.

MACGILL. Good-bye; good-bye.

[*Mrs. Nethercliff opens the door and Elsie, followed to the door by Harmer, passes her and disappears.*

MRS. NETHERCLIFF. [*Hastening after Elsie.*] Elsie, you're not taking a sunshade! You'll be scorched to a cinder!

ELSIE. Oh, and a good job too, aunt!

MRS. NETHERCLIFF. [*Out of sight.*] Darling—! [*The front-door slams.*] Oh—! [*To Harmer.*] Walter——!

HARMER. [*Soothingly.*] All right, auntie; don't fret. Elsie's beauty is more than skin-deep. [*He nods to her and then closes the door of the room softly and crosses to the fireplace.*] That poor kid's nerves are on edge. Auntie means well, but she's been getting rather a fidget lately. [*MacGill, who has wandered meditatively to the back of the room, comes forward.*] Phew! [*Smiling.*] We shall both be jolly glad—Elsie and I—we shall both be jolly glad when we're through with it.

MACGILL. Married and done for?

HARMER. And find ourselves trudging up the grassy slopes at Wengen, and rambling in the pinewoods!

MACGILL. Wengen—Switzerland——?

HARMER. [*Throwing his arms in the air.*] Switzerland! Switzerland! [*With a change of tone—going to MacGill.*] MacGill——

MACGILL. Yes?

HARMER. I'm an awful cadger—will you do August for me again this year? The whole of it—not a day short——!

MACGILL. [*Holding the lapel of Harmer's jacket.*] Why, what d'ye think I'm here for this afternoon——?

HARMER. No——!

MACGILL. Merely to announce my return to civilization?

HARMER. You *will*——!

MACGILL. I've come over specially to offer my invaluable services.

HESTON & ISLEWORTH DISTRICT
HOUNSLOW
PUBLIC LIBRARIES

HARMER. [*Wringing MacGill's hand.*] My dear fellow! My dear, dear fellow——!

MACGILL. Tcht, tcht, tcht! [*Withdrawing his hand and putting it behind him.*] The thirty-first of July is the date of the interesting ceremony, isn't it?

HARMER. Thursday, July the thirty-first, two o'clock. The usual gathering afterwards; lord ha' mercy on us! We shall have to get away soon, though, to catch the half-past four from Victoria. We stay the night at Dover. [*Putting an arm round MacGill's shoulders and speaking with a mixture of lightness and feeling.*] Mac —excuse my gross familiarity—Mac, I don't want to talk platitudes——

MACGILL. [*Jokingly.*] Oh, pray don't condemn yourself to silence.

HARMER. [*Punching him in the chest.*] You cold-blooded wretch, you! [*Leaving him and walking about the room on the left.*] Mac, there's a period in the fortunes of most men—the undeserving as well as the deserving—when the sky above them hasn't the sign of a fleck in it, and the barometer is set so steadily at "fair" that it's hard to believe that it'll ever vary. [*Pulling himself up and grinning at MacGill.*] Mac, that's where *I* am at this moment!

MACGILL. [*Still jesting.*] Ugh! Make the most of your blue sky, my lad. [*Harmer resumes his walk by marching to and fro at the back of the room.*] I advise you to make the most of it, and not to tap the weather-glass.

HARMER. [*Laughing.*] Curmudgeon!

MACGILL. [*Strolling across to the left, where he casu-*

*ally examines a piece of music lying on the top of the piano.*] The future; what are your plans? Do you hang on where you are?

HARMER. Yes. I'm buying the lease from Mrs. Nethercliff; twenty-three years unexpired. Auntie will continue to live with us; in the beginning, to spare Elsie. My little wife won't be equal to the toil of housekeeping yet awhile. [*Halting at the round table.*] And I'm re-furnishing the rooms upstairs and making 'em pretty. The walls of Elsie's room are to be dove-grey, and the curtains rose-coloured silk with a lining of rich cream. [*Sitting at the table and drumming upon it.*] And I've ordered a new car—a Talbot coupé—eighteen horse-power—the body dark brown picked out in dull red. My old tin-kettle of a two-seater isn't fit for Elsie to drive. And I—[*breaking off and holding out his hand to MacGill*] Mac, it was you who brought me to this house, fixed me up here with Mrs. Nethercliff. [*As MacGill goes to him.*] I don't forget what I owe to you, and never shall; never.

MACGILL. [*Giving Harmer's hand a quick but warm shake.*] Mrs. Nethercliff and Elsie also owe me something on that score, I reckon. [*Resting his hand on Harmer's shoulder.*] Walter—excuse my gross familiarity —Walter, with all my heart, the best of luck to you!

HARMER. [*Looking up at him.*] Thank you, Mac; thank you, with all my heart.

[*MacGill is turning away when he pauses for an instant with a twinkle in his eye, as if a humorous thought had occurred to him.*

MACGILL. By-the-bye, have you ever seen or heard anything more of the poor devil who told you that ugly story about himself—the highly respectable bloke who couldn't resist going on the randan occasionally? [*Getting no answer.*] *You* remember?

HARMER. [*Raising his head slowly, his face a blank, and looking at MacGill again.*] The highly respectable—? [*Shaking his head.*] No, I—I don't remember.

MACGILL. You don't! [*Prompting Harmer's memory.*] Last year—when we were having tea together—the day before you started on your holiday—you were giving me an instance——

HARMER. [*Calmly.*] Ah, yes, I—I recollect. No, I haven't seen or heard from him since. Why—why do you ask?

MACGILL. [*Chuckling.*] Ha, ha, ha! Ho, ho, ho! [*Slapping Harmer on the back.*] I *must* chuck it off my chest. Walter, for half a minute I had a suspicion that you were telling your *own* story; I had indeed. Ha, ha, ha—! [*He checks his merriment as Harmer, with a haughty expression, gets to his feet.*] I beg your pardon, old chap. You're not offended?

HARMER. [*Stiffly.*] My—my own story——?

MACGILL. You were so desperately in earnest—laid the paint on so thick. You ought to write one of these sensation novels, 'pon my word you ought—a picture on the cover, showing the unfortunate fellow—! [*Harmer turns from MacGill and, with head erect, walks to the fireplace. MacGill follows him for a few steps.*] Oh, damn it all, man, don't be shirty over a trifle! I needn't have said anything about it! Walter——!

[*There is a brief silence, during which neither stirs, and then Harmer faces MacGill.*

HARMER. [*In a voice that is not much above a whisper.*] MacGill——

MACGILL. [*Startled by the alteration in Harmer's manner.*] Eh?

HARMER. I'll be honest with you, MacGill; I'll be honest with you. It *was* my own story I told you that afternoon; it was my own story.

MACGILL. [*Staring at Harmer.*] It *was!*

HARMER. [*Taking out his handkerchief and wiping his lips.*] Oh, yes, you were right in suspecting that I was giving myself away. It *was* my own story; my own story to the letter.

MACGILL. [*Puckering his mouth.*] Well, there's no necessity to give yourself away any further, Harmer. [*Retreating a little.*] To be candid, I—[*with a sniff*] I'd rather you didn't.

HARMER. [*Pleadingly.*] Oh, but I'm owning up to what belongs to the *past*, MacGill; to a past that's as dead as the driest skeleton under the earth. What you see to-day is my *real* self—the self I always aimed at being—the self I always, always aimed at being—not the wretched, despicable creature I described to you. [*Sitting on the settee and rolling his handkerchief into a ball between the palms of his hands.*] MacGill— MacGill, don't scoff at me for trying to introduce a touch of romance into my miserable record——

MACGILL. [*Hardly repressing a sneer.*] Romance——?

HARMER. [*Gazing into space.*] You know the legend —the old legend of the blasphemer who incurred the wrath of God—whose only chance of salvation lay in his winning the love of a good, pure girl? Sometimes, thinking things over, I fancy there's a similarity between my case and that fable.

MACGILL. [*Moving to the smoking-table and from there surveying Harmer coldly.*] Elsie—you're alluding to little Elsie?

HARMER. [*Nodding.*] To Elsie. [*Rubbing his knees thoughtfully.*] Oh, I don't say that I've won her love yet completely. That'll grow—that'll come later on, when she realises how deep my devotion is, how thorough, how patient. [*Turning to MacGill.*] MacGill, you must admit it *is* strange; there *is* romance in it?

MACGILL. [*Under his breath, gruffly.*] Umph——!

HARMER. A few weeks ago my affection for Elsie was simply an ordinary affection for a child who happened to be living under the same roof with me—a child in whose welfare one was obliged to concern oneself as for a member of one's family. And then, in a second, the accident of Birkett giving her the push changes our relationship, and it's she who steps out of a cloud, as it were, and lifts the curse from me; it's she who lifts the curse from me! [*Springing up.*] Oh, I—I don't know what's possessed me to lay myself bare to you in this way. I suppose you'll never be more than commonly civil to me henceforth. [*Entreatingly.*] MacGill! M-Mac!

MACGILL. [*Almost groaning.*] Harmer—Harmer——

HARMER. W-w-well——?

MACGILL. I wish to heaven you *hadn't* unloaded this on me. Why the deuce couldn't you have held your tongue! Why——?

[*The door on the left opens and Harmer restrains MacGill by a gesture. Mrs. Nethercliff enters quietly and, with a half-scared look, stands near the door without further movement.*

HARMER. [*After waiting for her to speak.*] Hallo! [*Mrs. Nethercliff rouses herself and softly closes the door.*] Anything the matter?

MRS. NETHERCLIFF. [*To MacGill, advancing a little.*] Excuse me. [*To Harmer.*] Walter——

HARMER. [*Quite composed again.*] Yes?

MRS. NETHERCLIFF. Elsie—Elsie has come back.

HARMER. Already?

MRS. NETHERCLIFF. N-not alone. She—she isn't alone.

HARMER. Who——?

MRS. NETHERCLIFF. She—she has brought Mr. Birkett with her.

HARMER. [*Incredulously.*] Birkett? [*Mrs. Nethercliff inclines her head.*] Brought Birkett with her?

MRS. NETHERCLIFF. She met him by chance at the corner of Dighton Road. [*Harmer goes to her.*] They've met before, it appears, when she's been out walking.

HARMER. [*Knitting his brows.*] They—they've met before——?

MRS. NETHERCLIFF. Once or twice.

HARMER. She hasn't mentioned it.

MRS. NETHERCLIFF. Not to me.

HARMER. What—what does Mr. Birkett want here?

MRS. NETHERCLIFF. An interview with you. He asks for an interview with you—now, if convenient—at which she may be present.

HARMER. Why? What's his object?

MRS. NETHERCLIFF. [*Faintly.*] I—I've no idea.

HARMER. Does—does Elsie——?

MRS. NETHERCLIFF. Yes; *she* wants you to see him, too.

HARMER. [*After considering for a moment.*] Oh, by all means. Will you—er——?

MACGILL. [*Coming to Harmer as Mrs. Nethercliff is moving absently to the door.*] Good-bye. I'll hook it.

HARMER. No, no; you must stop and have some tea— mustn't he, auntie? [*Going to the folding-doors.*] Wait here.

[*MacGill joins him and Mrs. Nethercliff goes out, shutting the door behind her.*

MACGILL. [*As Harmer is opening the leaf of the folding-doors.*] H'm! Confounded cheek, Harmer, on Mr. Birkett's part, whatever his motive!

HARMER. I agree. [*MacGill passes into the consulting-room.*] Smoke your pipe; the fumes'll go out o' the window.

[*Having closed the leaf of the doors, he returns to the fireplace and there stands eyeing the door on the left. As he does so, his face takes on a look of fear and becomes lined and aged. In a little while the door is opened timidly by*

85

*Elsie and she creeps in followed by Birkett.
She is without her hat, but Birkett is carrying
his, clutched in nervous hands.*

BIRKETT. [*Passing Elsie and advancing to the farther
side of the round table—twisting his hat about.*] Good
afternoon, doctor.

HARMER. [*With a nod—his face clearing.*]   Good
afternoon.

BIRKETT. Very—very kind of you to see me——

HARMER. Not at all; not at all.

BIRKETT. Exceedingly kind.

HARMER. [*Airily.*]  To employ a popular formula, to
what do I owe the pleasure of this visit, Birkett?

BIRKETT. [*Moving a step towards Harmer.*] Frankly,
I—I am at a loss how to—how to begin exactly——

ELSIE. [*Who has shut the door and joined Birkett—
sinking into the chair at the round table.*]  Oh, please
don't be angry with us! Please, please don't be angry
with us!

HARMER. [*Raising his eyebrows.*] Angry——?

BIRKETT. Harmer, can't you guess why Elsie and I
present ourselves to you like this?  Surely you can
guess?

HARMER. [*Hunching his shoulders negatively.*] Afraid
I can't.

ELSIE. [*Leaning her head on her hands.*]  Walter—
Walter—I—I confess: I've been meeting Oswald out of
doors lately—I've met him two or three times——

BIRKETT. [*Correcting her.*]  Four times. counting to-
day——

86

ELSIE. I've tried to avoid him; indeed I have—tried my hardest——

BIRKETT. Not harder than I; not harder than I, to find strength to avoid Elsie!

ELSIE. That's why I've cooped myself up in the house —refused to go for walks. Simply to dodge Oswald!

BIRKETT. The first time we met, after our separation —[to Elsie] where was it?——

ELSIE. Frogmore Vale——

BIRKETT. Yes, yes; Frogmore Vale——

ELSIE. [To Harmer.] We were on opposite sides of the road, and I didn't mean to take the slightest notice of him; but somehow we stopped, and I strolled over to him. And then I got frightened we'd be observed, and I made an appointment to meet him next evening near the Reservoir. It was entirely my fault——

BIRKETT. No, no——

ELSIE. [Beating the table.] It was; it was. [Weakly.] I seemed to have so much to say, and I—I hadn't finished——

HARMER. [Sternly, to both of them.] At any rate, you did meet at the Reservoir——

ELSIE. Not that evening. I didn't keep the appointment.

BIRKETT. I waited an hour for her—longer——

ELSIE. I didn't keep the appointment and determined never to speak another syllable to him under any circumstances. But after a few days out I went again, hoping I should come across him, yet hoping, hoping, hoping I shouldn't  And at last, quite a fortnight later, not having seen him, I yielded to temptation and sped off to the Reservoir. Old Nick whispered to me that Oswald would be there; and, lo and behold, there he was!

BIRKETT. I'd fallen into the sinful habit of going up there every evening I was free, thinking that, after all, Elsie would come.

ELSIE. And it was then, while we were sheltering from the rain—it had set in beastly wet—it was then the truth dawned on us.

HARMER. The truth——?

ELSIE. [*To Birkett.*] Oswald——!

[*Birkett raises and drops his arms helplessly.*

HARMER. [*Sharply.*] The truth——?

ELSIE. That, notwithstanding what had occurred, we —Oswald and I—we still wished to marry each other, Walter.

[*A dead silence ensues, without a movement from anybody, and then Harmer turns his back upon Birkett and Elsie and seats himself in the chair facing the fireplace.*

BIRKETT. [*After a further pause—to Elsie.*] The rest—the rest— [*walking away from her*] the rest, Elsie.

ELSIE. [*In a plaintive voice.*] *You,* Oswald——!

BIRKETT. [*Steadying himself and halting by the writing-table.*] We met once more at the Reservoir, Harmer —once more—to confirm our resolve to pursue a righteous line of conduct, and to say farewell. [*Throwing his hat upon the table.*] It is due to both of us that I

should make that clear to you. We had no intention—
solemnly I affirm it—no desire to act treacherously towards you. I recognised—tardily, alas!—I recognised
that I am the merest flesh and blood, and that in seek-
ing in the name of religion to close my ears to the call of
my manhood I had been guilty of arrogance and vain-
glory. Nevertheless we bowed our heads to the penalty
my vacillation—my shilly-shallying—exacted from us
and, irrevocably, as we believed, we did say good-bye.
[*Dropping into the chair at the writing-table in a woe-
begone attitude.*] And that would have been the end of
it, Harmer, if Elsie and I hadn't been destined to run
against one another in Dighton Road just now.

ELSIE. [*Rising and going to Birkett.*] Oswald had
arranged to go away to-morrow, and to remain away till
after my marriage.

BIRKETT. Yes, I've taken a lodging at Herne Bay.
[*Producing a letter from his pocket-book.*] I can show
you a letter from the landlady, to prove my good faith.
[*Elsie takes the letter from him and reads it.*] James
Pankridge, of Wandsworth, a truly inspired preacher
and a worthier man than I, has consented to fill my
place during my absence.

ELSIE. [*Reading the letter aloud.*] " 5, Esplanade,
Herne Bay, June 22nd. Dear Sir, I am reserving the
rooms for you from Thursday the twenty-sixth——"
[*Going to Harmer and standing at the back of his chair.*]
You can see for yourself, Walter, how straight Oswald
has tried to be.

BIRKETT. [*Sitting upright.*] Elsie and I, obviously,

have had only a hurried, impulsive talk. We are swept to you on the flood-tide of our emotion, so to speak.

ELSIE. Our brains are in a whirl, naturally.

BIRKETT. If we had delayed approaching you till we were more collected, the burden of our appeal would have been the same. Forgiveness—toleration—compassion! [*Starting up and walking about.*] We throw ourselves on your compassion, Harmer; we throw ourselves on your compassion. Bestow it, and, in the words of the gospel, you will lay up for yourself treasures in heaven!

ELSIE. [*Whimpering.*] I'm afraid I only promised to marry you out of pique, Walter, fond as I am of you; but, of course, if you hold me to my bargain, it would be rotten of me to turn you down. I'm not such a cad as that.

BIRKETT. [*Joining Elsie.*] Our fate, Harmer, as far as it can be in mortal hands, is in yours. We await your sentence.

ELSIE. Like criminals——

[*Harmer, who has been sitting quiescently staring at the flowers on the hearth, slowly gets to his feet and confronts the pair. He is quite calm and there is a smile on his lips.*

HARMER. [*Very gently.*] Sentence? You await *my* sentence? Why, Elsie—why, Birkett—it seems to me that you are pronouncing sentence upon *me*.

ELSIE. [*Feebly protesting.*] Oh, Walter——!

HARMER. [*Checking her.*] Yes, yes, yes, I understand; [*drawing a deep breath*] I understand. [*Leaving them and straying to the other side of the room—speaking more to himself than to them.*] Pique—humiliation—injured pride—as if I don't know what drove you to me; as if I don't know! [*At the left of the round table, his eyes on the ground, his smile lingering—tapping the table softly.*] Still, marriages have been successful, starting under much less favourable auspices than ours would, Elsie. The devotion—the ceaseless devotion of the husband—*that* touches a woman in the long run, old lady, doesn't it? [*Her head drooping, and with a little wriggle of her shoulder-blades, Elsie moves to the fireplace. Birkett follows her, biting his moustache.*] But look here. [*He goes to them and holds out his hands to the girl. Turning her face from him and pouting, she puts her hand in his.*] Look here. [*Tenderly.*] I want you to be happy, my dear; I want you to be happy. [*Giving his left hand to Birkett while retaining Elsie's.*] And I bear no ill-will to Birkett; not a scrap.

BIRKETT. [*Thickly.*] Thank you, Harmer; I—I thank you.

HARMER. [*Releasing their hands after a final shake—in a wistful tone.*] Perhaps you might have given the matter a little more consideration; just a little more. As you've said, your talk, since you butted into one another in Dighton Road, has been a very hurried one. [*Going to the folding-doors.*] However, I won't murmur. [*Turning to them, his hand on the door-handle.*] Tell Mrs. Nethercliff the upshot of the affair, will you, and say that I—that I'm a mass of amiability about it.

[*Looking at Elsie.*] I want you to be happy, old lady. [*Opening the leaf of the folding-doors.*] S'long, both of you!

    [*He goes into the consulting-room, closing the leaf of the folding-doors behind him. There is a short pause, and then Elsie, with a disconsolate air, walks away from Birkett.*

ELSIE. [*Her mouth twitching.*] So that's over!

BIRKETT. [*Following her—heavily.*] Yes—over.

ELSIE. [*Swallowing her tears.*] I wish—I wish to goodness—he'd raved and stormed at me. [*Clenching her fists and stamping.*] Why the hell couldn't he have raved and stormed at me, instead of—! [*Seeing Birkett's look of horror.*] Sorry. But he keeps on declaring that he wants me to be happy, and then he does his best to make me utterly miserable.

BIRKETT. [*Pressing his hands to his temples.*] He has behaved splendidly—splendidly.

ELSIE. [*Finding she is clutching the letter from Herne Bay, and returning it to him.*] I suppose you'll chuck Herne Bay now, Oswald, won't you, and stick to me?

BIRKETT. Certainly. I'll write to Mrs.—[*referring to the letter*] Mrs. Nuttall—at once and send her some money; [*cramming the letter into his breast-pocket*] and I'll communicate with Pankridge.

ELSIE. [*Fetching his hat.*] Run away. *I'll* tackle aunt. I'd rather cope with her alone. [*Opening the door on the left.*] You shall hear from me in the morning how things are.

[*He takes her head between his hands and mutters a blessing; then she gives him his hat and he passes her and speaks to her from the doorway.*

BIRKETT. I shall be at home to-night, in case you should need me.

ELSIE. Right'o.

[*He disappears and, leaning against the doorpost, she watches him let himself out. Presently the front-door slams, and then she wanders dejectedly to the middle of the room and stands gazing at the folding-doors. In a moment or two Mrs. Nethercliff steals along the passage and peeps in.*

MRS. NETHERCLIFF. [*In a hushed voice.*] Elsie——

ELSIE. [*Starting.*] Oh—! [*Dully.*] Yes, aunt?

MRS. NETHERCLIFF. [*Casting a backward glance at the front-door as she enters.*] Mr. Birkett has gone?

ELSIE. Just departed.

MRS. NETHERCLIFF. [*Advancing.*] Well? Have you anything to tell me?

ELSIE. Only that Oswald and I are engaged again, auntie.

MRS. NETHERCLIFF. [*Bowing her head.*] I knew it. I knew it. Where's Walter?

ELSIE. [*Pointing to the folding-doors.*] In there.

MRS. NETHERCLIFF. [*Looking at Elsie steadily.*] The best man that's ever lived, Elsie.

ELSIE. [*Nodding.*] Yes, auntie. [*Crossing to the door on the left.*] I don't want any tea; I'm going to bed.

[*At the door.*] May Ida bring me up a bowl of bread-and-milk by-and-by?

MRS. NETHERCLIFF. Yes, darling.

[*Elsie goes out, shutting the door.*

MRS. NETHERCLIFF. [*Almost inaudibly.*] My boy— my boy—my boy——! [*She raps softly on the leaf of the folding-doors.*

## THE SEVENTH SCENE

*Outside Mrs. Nethercliff's house again, the light as before.*

> [*Harmer comes out, carrying his bag and dressed very much as when he left the house in the Second Scene. Repeating the action of that scene with but little variance, he steals away into the gloom.*

# THE EIGHTH SCENE

*Lilian Dipple's lodging again, everything being much
the same as it was nearly twelve months ago. The
time is about ten o'clock at night and the room is
poorly lighted by a bluish jet of flame sprouting
from the nipple of the gas-bracket. Stretched
across the window from one rusty nail to another
is the piece of sacking; but as it hardly reaches the
top of the window, the upper sash is seen to be
lowered. In the court the faint gleam of a street-
lamp mingles with what is left of daylight.*

*On the table are the remnants of a meal—the
heel of a german-sausage, an empty beer-jug and
tumbler, some bread and cheese and margarine,
and a plate and a knife.*

*Lilian's walking-shoes are lying on the floor near
the wicker chair. The bed is partially disarranged,
as if somebody has been resting upon it.*

[*Lilian is standing in the middle of the room getting
into a bedraggled skirt which may once have
been of a gay pattern. She is already attired
in a flashy blouse and is freshly painted for
her night's prowl. Having fastened the waistband of her skirt, she goes to the wicker chair,
kicks off her slippers and, sitting in the chair,
picks up her walking-shoes and puts them on.
She has just finished tying their laces when*

*there is a loud and agitated knocking at the door.*

LILIAN. [*Almost jumping out of her skin.*] Ow, Chri—! [*She scurries to the door and opens it a little way and peers into the darkness.*] 'Oo is it?

FLORENCE. [*Tremulously.*] Yew b'yerself, Lil?

LILIAN. [*Still blocking up the entrance.*] Yus.

FLORENCE. Lem'me in! F'r Gawd'saike, lem'me in! [*Pushing past Lilian and staggering towards the fireplace.*] Lem'me in, carn't yer!

LILIAN. [*Shutting the door and going to Florence.*] Wot's the matter, knockin' the bleedin' 'ouse dahn?

FLORENCE. [*Whose face is white and pinched and who is shaking like a person with the ague.*] Oh, Lil; oh, my gal! Wotyer think; I gotter go inter the 'orspital!

LILIAN. 'Orspital!

FLORENCE. Inter Guy's 'Orspital.

LILIAN. Wot for?

FLORENCE. [*Clinging to her.*] Oh, I bin in sech dre'-ful p'ine, Lil! I bin feelin' strainge in me inside f'r evers'long, an' this evenin' I was took reg'ler bad, an' me lan'lidy's son rushed aht an' fetched a doctor t'me, an' the ol' man mauled me abaht an' sez I'm a urgent caise.

LILIAN. [*Wide-eyed.*] H'urgent!

FLORENCE. 'E 'phoned ter the 'orspital ter arrainge f'me goin' in, an' I'm on me w'y theer nah. [*She leaves Lilian and sinks into the wicker chair and rocks herself to and fro.*] Oh! Oh, my Gawd, Lil! Me! Me! Fancee me bein' a urgent caise!

LILIAN. [*In a scared voice, pointing to a dirty newspaper parcel which Florence is hugging tightly.*] Wot-yer got'n that parsul?

FLORENCE. [*Leaning back and closing her eyes.*] It's the things I'm re-quired ter taike inter the 'orspital. They ain't 'arf fussy, these yere 'orspitals, I mus' s'y! The doctor give me the list. Two tow'ls, me brush-an'-comb, a caike o' soap an' a toothbrush, an' a couple o' nightgowns. As true as 'eaven's above us, Lil, I've 'ad ter buy a toothbrush an' a couple o' nightgowns! [*Opening her eyes to find that Lilian is staring at her.*] Yew—yew don' b'lieve theer's enny feer o' me dyin', do yer? [*Struggling into an upright position.*] Lil—Lil—! [*With sudden fierceness.*] Curse yer f'r a 'ard-'arted bitch, don' stan' lookin' at me as if yer thought theer was a charnce o' me dyin'!

LILIAN. [*Rallying her.*] Yew! Ho, ho! *Yew* die! Not *yew!*

FLORENCE. [*Subsiding again and blubbering.*] Huh! huh! huh! I want yer ter come ter the 'orspital with me, Lil, an' st'y with me till they put me ter bed; will yer, deerie? I wan'ter show 'em I ain't alone in the world—show 'em I got nice frien's. [*Beseechingly.*] Yer will, woncher?

LILIAN. Corse. [*Going to the row of hooks on the right of the door.*] No trouble ter *me*. I was jes' start-in' aht.

FLORENCE. Me lan'lidy orferred ter come, but I h'upset 'er with me moanin' an' 'ollerin' an' she's as drunk as a owl.

LILIAN. [*Who has unhooked a crushed piece of finery bearing some resemblance to a hat—punching its crown into shape.*] Luckee I was laite ter-night! I bin layin' dahn on me bed an' I h'overslep' meself. [*There is a gentle rapping of the door-knocker. She pauses, listening.*] Ullo—? [*Tossing the hat on to the bed, she opens the door and peeps out as before.*] Yus?

GORHAM. G'd evenin', Miss Dipple. 'Ope I ain't introodin'.

LILIAN. [*Not very cordially.*] Alf?

GORHAM. D'yer 'appen ter be disingaiged, m'y I arsk?

LILIAN. Wot's that t'yew?

GORHAM. Need'n' be so 'uffy. [*Gradually worming himself into the room in spite of Lilian's reluctance to admit him.*] I brought an' ol' frien' ter see yer. We bin 'untin' f'yer all over the pl'ice—the " Lord Nelson "— the " H'Earl Grey "——

LILIAN. Ol' frien'? Wot ol' frien'?

GORHAM. [*To Florence, who makes no response.*] G'd evenin', Miss Portch. [*Opening the door fully and calling softly to somebody on the landing.*] Hi! Mister—! [*Harmer appears in the doorway. His face is moist and waxen, his lids are heavy, and he is rather unsteady in his gait. He and Lilian gaze at each other without speaking, he with a vacant smile, she with a puzzled frown.*] Yew remember the gen'leman, don'yer, Miss Dipple?

LILIAN. [*Running her eye over Harmer dubiously.*] G'd evenin'.

HARMER. [*Thickly.*] How d'ye do?

LILIAN. 'Ave I h'ever seen yer be-fore?

GORHAM. [*Highly amused.*] Ho, ho! I like that! 'Ave yew ever see the gen'leman be-fore! Ho, ho, ho——!

HARMER. [*Taking his hat off.*] Yes; d-d-don't you recollec'? Las' year—I stayed with you two'r s'hree weeks——

LILIAN. [*Suddenly seizing his hand and shaking it heartily.*] Gaw'bli'me, sh'd think I do rec'lec'! [*She leads him into the room and Gorham closes the door.*] Yor the gen'lemen wot useter gim'me fl'ar's!

HARMER. [*Nodding.*] L-L-Lilian your name is——

LILIAN. That's right. [*Pulling him towards her.*] 'Ere! Don'yer wanner kiss me——?

[*They exchange kisses.*

GORHAM. [*Rubbing his hands.*] Ho, ho, ho——!

LILIAN. [*Taking Harmer's hat and bag from him.*] Gim'me yer truck. Y'goin' ter st'y with me ag'ine, ain't yer?

HARMER. If you—if you'll let me.

[*She stands his bag on the trunk at the foot of the bed and hangs his hat on one of the hooks which are on the wall between the bed and the door.*

GORHAM. [*Sitting in the chair at the farther side of the table.*] Me an' the boys was 'avin' a drink at the "Crahn an' Anker" an' in the gen'leman walked.

[*Lilian returns to Harmer and helps him out of his overcoat.*] Yer mighter knocked us all dahn with a feather. 'E reckernised us at once't. Kin yew tell me, 'e said—after we'd 'ad a prelim'ary talk—kin yew tell me, 'e said, w'ere the young party lives I maide the acquinetance of lars summer—it's clean gorn ahter me nut, 'e said—[*His attention is attracted by Florence who again has her eyes shut and is rolling from side to side.*] Ain't yer well, Miss Portch?

LILIAN. [*Who has hung up the coat on another of the hooks—coming to Gorham with her hat in her hand.*] No, she ain't. She's gotter go inter th' 'orspital, Flo 'as.

GORHAM. 'Orspital!

LILIAN. Inter Guy's 'orspital. [*Putting on her hat.*] I'm taikin' 'er theer nah, an' I'm goin' ter w'ite till they put 'er inter 'er bed.

GORHAM. [*Mournfully.*] Oh, deer, oh, deer! Wotter bad job!

[*Harmer has now become aware of the presence of Florence, and at the mention of the hospital has moved towards her.*

LILIAN. [*To Harmer.*] Yew re-member Flo—Flo Portch? [*At his elbow.*] G'arn! Don' s'y yer don't, 'cos yer do!

HARMER. [*Blinking at Florence.*] Yes—yes——

FLORENCE. [*Raising herself with an effort.*] G'd evenin', mister.

HARMER. [*Touching her shoulder.*] I—I'm sor'y t'hear you're ill; ve'y sor'y indeed. [*Mechanically he*

*runs his hand down her arm, and his fingers close upon
her wrist.*] How—how're you going t'get t'the hospital?

> [*Lilian, Florence, and Gorham look on in mute
> astonishment while he counts the rate of
> Florence's pulse. At length, unable to restrain
> her curiosity, Lilian plucks at his sleeve.*

LILIAN. 'Ere! I s'y! Er yew a doctor?

HARMER. [*Dropping Florence's hand.*] I! [*Shaking
his head.*] N-no. N-no.

LILIAN. Wotyer feelin' 'er pulse for, then?

HARMER. [*Sharply—trying to pull himself together.*]
How're you going to get to the hospital, you women?

LILIAN. [*Still wondering.*] On ahr shanks, I s'pose
—[*divining his intention*] h'unless yer mean ter stan'
us a taxee.

> [*He takes his note-case, bulging with paper-money,
> from his breast-pocket and gives Lilian a
> pound note. Then, finding Florence's hand
> outstretched, he gives her also a note.*

FLORENCE. [*Grabbing at it and thrusting it into her
bodice.*] Thank'yer, mister; thank'yer.

LILIAN. [*Folding her note.*] Ain't rode'n taxee f'r
h'aiges. [*She is tucking her note into her stocking,
below a ragged garter, when she sees that Gorham has
risen and is watching Harmer with greedy eyes. She
turns quickly to Harmer, who is fiddling with the notes
in his case, and, gripping his hand, forces him to re-
place the case in his pocket.*] Ah-h-h-h, yer sillee fool,
yeh! Flashin' yer money abaht that w'y! Yew de-serve
ter 'ave yer pockits gutted, yew do! [*She stands pant-*

*ing for a moment; then, wiping the sweat from her throat with the back of her hand, she sweeps to the door and opens it.*] Well, much erblige t'yer, Alf, f'r bringin' th' gen'leman erlong. Des's'y we sh'll be seein' yer termorrer somew'eres.

GORHAM. [*A little reluctantly.*] I'm shore I 'ope so, Miss Dipple; I'm shore I 'ope so. [*Grasping Harmer's hand.*] Please ter meet yer ag'ine, guv'ner; an' so's them boys—so's George Kelk an' young Perce, pore aht-o'-works.

HARMER. Thank you.

GORHAM. I wish yer goo'-night.

HARMER. Good night.

GORHAM. [*To Florence.*] Yew too, Miss Portch. [*She gives him a glassy look in acknowledgment.*] Yor goin' inter th' 'orspital remin's me o'my unforchnit missus—[*Lilian rattles the handle of the latch*] comin' Miss Dipple. [*As he passes Lilian.*] Goo' night t'yer.

LILIAN. [*Following him to the landing.*] Goo' night. [*Gorham disappears and she returns and shuts the door. In the meantime Harmer has wandered across the room and is contemplating in a sickly way the remains of the meal on the table.*] W'ere'd I leave me key? [*She finds it beside the candlestick on the orange-box. It is attached to a circle of dirty ribbon.*] 'Ere 'tis. [*Slipping the ribbon over her head and dropping the key into her bosom, she goes to Harmer.*] Sharn't be more'n an ahr, I 'spect, at the ahtside. Maike yerself at 'ome, woncher? Wotyer squintin' at?

HARMER. Hungry—I'm hungry, Lilian——

LILIAN. 'Ungry?

HARMER. Faint. Nothing to eat since five o'clock this morning. Roll'n' butter at a coffee-stall.

LILIAN. Five er-clock——?

HARMER. I gave a girl her dinner at a shop in the Cut, but I only shared her drink.

LILIAN. [*Pointing to the scraps on the table.*] Theer's a bit o' sossidge lef' fr'm me supper, an' some bread'n' cheese'n' marge. Kin yer do with that, deerie? [*Bustling to the cupboard.*] 'Ere! I gotter clean pl'ite in 'ere—

HARMER. [*While she is rummaging for the plate.*] Don't bother. I'll go out with you and—[*glancing at Florence*] and Flo—and get some food while you're at the hospital.

LILIAN. [*Turning to him, the plate in her hand.*] No, yer won't! Yew don' go aht ag'ine ter-night, nor ter-morrer withaht me! [*Placing the clean plate on the table and removing the dirty one.*] Sit dahn. [*He sits obediently at the farther side of the table.*] P'r'aps I'll bring some jellied h'eels in with me, if I come acrost enny. [*Putting the dirty plate on the top of the cupboard with a clatter and searching in the cupboard again.*] W'y ye'd be bahned ter fall in with them boys ag'ine if I let yer aht!

HARMER. [*Sawing away at the sausage.*] They wouldn't harm me, those fellows. No' they!

LILIAN. Don' mean yer ter taike no risks. [*Throwing a crooked two-pronged, black-handled fork on to the table.*] Tell yer theer was a re-spectable bloke murdered close by 'ere yeers ago—gen'leman, jes' like yew—

an' by igsac'ly th' saime clarss as Alf Gorham an' 'is pals.

HARMER. [*Beginning to eat.*] Years ago——!

[*The sound of the playing of the concertina in the court steals softly in at the window.*

FLORENCE. 'Fore I was born, but we don' chainge much'n this part o' the tahn.

HARMER. [*Listening to the concertina as he munches and beating time to the tune with his knife.*] A'ha! Th' ol' music! Th' ol' music!

LILIAN. [*Resting her hands on the table and leaning over it to watch him eat.*] Yus, they took the gen'le-man—'e was lushy, saime as wot yew are—they took 'im, I've 'eard s'y, up a dark passidge be'ind the "George the Fourth" publ'ykouse, an' did 'im in. Theer was three of 'em in it. One planted 'isself at the h'entrance o' th' passidge, keepin' caivey, w'ile the others did the job. They was tried at the Ol' B'iley, but they was'n' 'ung f'r it. The jooree brought it in man-slaughter, 'cos the loryers mine-tained that the gen'le-man 'ad bin throttled by h'accident. [*Straightening herself.*] Shows yer, does'n' it?

HARMER. [*His mouth full.*] Ho! If I were set on by any of that lot, I think I'd manage to surprise 'em, Lilian.

LILIAN. [*Leering at him with half-shut eyes.*] B'lieve yer would, saucee! [*Closing the cupboard door, which she has left open.*] Theer's a drop o' strong in 'ere. We'll drink ahr 'ealths d'rec'lee I git back. [*Going to Florence.*] Readee, Flo? Flo! [*Shaking her gently.*] Waike up!

FLORENCE. [*Rousing herself.*] Yus, I—I—I'm readee.
[*As Lilian is helping Florence to her feet, the light
begins to grow dimmer.*

LILIAN. [*Scowling at the gas-burner.*] Blarst! Theer
goes the gess! [*To Harmer.*] Got a pennee on yer?

HARMER. [*Feeling in his trousers' pocket.*] Yes.

LILIAN. [*Jerking her head towards the meter as she
leads Florence to the door.*] Shove it in the slot, will yer?

HARMER. [*Rising to shake hands with Florence.*]
Good-bye. I hope you'll soon be out and about again.

FLORENCE. Oh, thank'yer, mister. [*Wailing.*] Oh—
oh—oh—oh——!

LILIAN. [*As Harmer goes to the door and opens it—
a note of tenderness in her roughness.*] G'arn! 'Old
yer rah! Aht an' abaht! Corse ye'll soon be aht an'
abaht. [*Putting her arm round Florence.*] 'Ere! I got
yer. I got yer, yer stoopid ol' cow——!

[*Harmer follows the two women to the landing
and watches them till they are out of sight;
then he comes back into the room and shuts
the door. He stands for a little while trying
to recollect what he has to do. The rapidly
fading light brings it to his mind and, with a
snap of the fingers, he turns to the gas-meter.
Discovering that the meter is beyond his
reach, he drags the chair which is on the right-
hand side of the bed to the meter, mounts the
chair with difficulty and, after some failures
owing to his unsteadiness, inserts his penny
in the slot. Then he dismounts and replaces*

*the chair and dances a few steps to the strains
of the concertina. The room becomes brighter
as he reseats himself at the table and resumes
eating. He has swallowed another mouthful
or two when it is borne in upon his muddled
brain that somebody is knocking at the door
very softly. He listens, and presently the
knocking is repeated; whereupon he rises and
opens the door and confronts Gorham. The
playing of the concertina stops.*

HARMER. Hallo! It's you again, is it?

GORHAM. I beg yer pard'n, mister——

HARMER. What's up?

GORHAM. I beg yer pard'n f'r th' lib'ty I'm taikin',
but it sud'nly come over me yew might be glad o' me
comp'ny ter 'elp pars the time w'ile Miss Dipple's at
the 'orspital.

HARMER. [*Allowing him to enter.*] S'tremely kind
of you.

GORHAM. [*Advancing.*] No fun, I sez t'meself, f'r a
gen'leman ter be settin' all alone in a 'umble erpart-
ment o' this sort—gen'leman 'oo resides mos' likely in
a fine 'ouse with 'ired servants at 'is beck an' call.

HARMER. [*Who has closed the door and returned to
the table—sitting and going on with his eating.*] Sor'y
I can't offer you any supper. I've nearly finished all
there is in the place.

GORHAM. [*Seating himself on the edge of the trunk
—ill at ease and with the tail of his eye roving nervously in the direction of the door.*] Oh, I 'ad me

supper orf three penn'orth o' cockles at a barr'er in the
Wart'loo Road, thank'yer jes' the saime, mister. Matt'r
o' fac', I—I was washin' it dahn with a pint o' st'art at
the " Crahn an' Anker " w'en yew—w'en yew——

    [*He breaks off, listening with strained ears. The
        playing of the concertina is resumed.*

    HARMER. [*Who, from his position at the table, has
his back to Gorham and the door—pushing his plate
from him.*] Phaugh! Glad you popped in. Glad you
popped in, Graham—Gorham. [*Looking at the window
and the wall surrounding it—drowsily.*] No, this isn't
a room one wants to be shut up in alone for long.
[*Waving an arm.*] The—the dec'rations might be im-
proved slightly, mightn't they?

    GORHAM. Y-yor right, mister, yor right; they might.
              [*Holding his breath, he gets to his feet.*

    HARMER. [*Maundering.*] The walls dove-grey—cur-
tains of rose-coloured silk—beau'iful rose-coloured silk
with a cream lining—that 'ud be an improvement,
wouldn't it?

    GORHAM. [*In a whisper, as he creeps to the door.*]
Yus, mister, yus; that 'ud be an im-provement.

    HARMER. [*His chin on his breast.*] Elsie's room—
dove-grey—rose-coloured silk curtains with a lining of
rich cream—lining of rich cream——

    [*Gorham opens the door noiselessly. Kelk and
        Crickmay are outside. He admits them and
        shuts the door; and then the three stand hud-
        dled together, looking at Harmer with evil
        faces.*

# THE NINTH SCENE

*The same, in great disorder, the gas still burning. The table is overturned, the things that were on it are scattered, and the three wooden chairs have been hurled about, one of them being in splinters. The piece of sacking, too, has been torn from the window, and there are other signs that a desperate struggle has taken place; and lying stark and stiff among the wreckage, with arms outspread and eyes staring upward, is Harmer's body.*

*After a short silence the shrill notes of the jig come from the court—the merry, mocking jig played on the concertina when it was first heard.*

THE END.

# CHILD MAN
## A SEDATE FARCE IN THREE ACTS

"Here I am on Tom Tiddler's Ground,
Picking up gold and silver."

*Old Nursery Rhyme.*

# THE PERSONS OF THE PLAY

### IN THE ORDER IN WHICH THEY APPEAR

IRENE (*a maidservant*).

MR. THRUPP (*of Odlum and Thrupp, House Agents*).

LORNA GILLBANKS.

COLIN MACCABE.

BRIAN (*aged ten*).

BETTY (*aged nine*).

ANTHONY GILLBANKS.

NUTT (*a gardener*).

JOAN (*the young lady next door*).

BETTY (*aged seventeen*).

BRIAN (*aged eighteen*).

GLADYS.

IVY. } (*Four Bright Young People*).

CLARENCE.

HAROLD.

LADY TORBRICK.

MARJORIE (*her daughter*).

MISS PLANT.

MR. BERKELEY SHRIMPTON (*a journalist*).

MISS VAN KOFF (*another*).

MR. INCE (*a photographer*).

HIS ASSISTANT.

MRS. LUMB (*housekeeper at the Beaufort Studios*).

EDITH (*her servant*).

# ACT I

EIGHT YEARS AGO.  MIMOSA ROAD, ST. JOHN'S WOOD.

# ACT II

THE PRESENT TIME.  STRAWBERRY GROVE, CHELSEA.

*Part I: Before the " At Home."   Part II: The end of the " At Home."*

# ACT III

BEAUFORT STUDIOS, TITUS STREET, CHELSEA.

*Part I: Evening of the same day.   Part II: The following morning.*

(N.B.—It is perhaps necessary to state that the various studios on the upper floors of this building are entered from a common stair, which is open to all comers until night-time without the intervention of a front-door.)

————

*The curtain falls between the Parts of Act II and Act III, but only for a little while.*

# THE FIRST ACT

*The scene—a triangular one, the apex of the triangle*
*being a little to the right of the centre of the stage*
*—represents a shabbily decorated and shabbily*
*furnished " drawing-room " in a small house in a*
*mean road in St. John's Wood.*

*In the left-hand wall there is a two-leaved window*
*opening to the floor.  Beyond is a poor little front-*
*garden, rank and weed-infested, edged with a row*
*of decaying shrubs and a groggy iron railing; and*
*beyond that is a view of the houses on the other*
*side of the road.*

*A door in the wall on the right opens into the*
*room from a passage leading from the front-door*
*to the rear of the house.  A hat-stand and a couple*
*of " hall " chairs are seen in the passage.*

*In the middle of the room, set to follow the line*
*of the wall on the left, there is a large settee; at*
*the right-hand end of the settee is a small round*
*table, and close to the table there is an arm-chair.*
*Another arm-chair stands on the right, but nearer*
*to the spectator and apart from the rest of the*
*furniture.*

*Against the wall between the door and the corner*
*of the room there is a bureau-bookcase; at the left-*
*hand side of the window are a small writing-table*
*and a chair; and on the extreme left of the room,*
*standing at right angles to the spectator, are a*
*cottage-piano and a four-legged music-stool.*

*The settee, the music-stool, and the chairs are covered with cretonne, and on the walls hang several water-colour drawings by that well-known artist Colin Maccabe in his earlier manner. A few cheap flowers, too, are placed about in vases; but the pattern of the cretonne is almost washed out, and the flowers are not over fresh, and altogether the attempts at embellishment accentuate rather than relieve the poverty-stricken appearance of the room.*

*The right-hand leaf of the window is open and the light outside is the glow of a fine August morning.*

(*Note: Throughout, "right" and "left" are the spectator's right and left, not the actor's.*)

[*Irene, a young "general" servant, flushed and untidy, enters from the passage. She is followed by Mr. Thrupp, who is without his hat but is evidently a caller.*

IRENE. [*As he passes her.*] Please wait a minute. I'll fetch Mrs. Gillbanks.

THRUPP. [*A middle-aged man of commercial aspect.*] No, no; it's Mr. Gillbanks I want.

IRENE. Sorry; Mr. Gillbanks is in his study. He never sees anybody when he's working.

THRUPP. Oh, all right; Mrs. Gillbanks, then.

[*Irene goes out and closes the door, whereupon Thrupp, keeping an eye on the door, moves about the room inspecting the various articles of furniture with a dubious air. Raising the lid of the piano he reads the name of the maker; then, pursing his lips and shaking his head gloomily, he shuts the piano and turns from it just in time to receive Lorna's salutation.*

LORNA. [*A bright, girlish young woman of nine-and-twenty, looking extremely personable in spite of the grubby, much-worn frock she is wearing.*] Good morning.

THRUPP. Good morning.

LORNA. [*Closing the door and advancing.*] How are you, Mr. Thrupp?

THRUPP. A I, thanks; hope you're the same.

LORNA. Pardon my raiment; you've caught me in my rags. Pray sit down. [*Winningly.*] What may I have the happiness of doing for you this fine day?

THRUPP. [*Seating himself on the settee in an uncomfortable attitude.*] Well, I——I don't want to worry you and your husband more than I can help, Mrs Gillbanks——

LORNA. [*Dropping into the arm-chair by the round table.*] *I* know! Don't say another word.

THRUPP. Unfortunately I must say another word——

LORNA. [*Wrinkling her nose.*] A word of four letters!

THRUPP. Four letters——?

LORNA. R-e-n-t.

THRUPP. [*With a nod.*] Rent.

LORNA. One letter for each beastly quarter.

THRUPP. And there are three owin'.

LORNA. Not yet.

THRUPP. Will be, the twenty-ninth of next month. Come now, we haven't been very troublesome, Mr. Odlum and I, have we?

LORNA. That you haven't; you've been perfect darlings.

THRUPP. Glad to hear your good opinion of us.

LORNA. And you'll continue to be indulgent to a poor author, won't you, Mr. Thrupp dear? Just a wee bit longer! For the sake of his peace of mind!

THRUPP. Yes, but what about *our* peace of mind? [*Changing his position on the settee.*] Your husband doesn't quite hit the mark with his littery work, I suppose?

LORNA. Depends on what you call the mark. If it's popular taste you mean, he doesn't try to hit the mark. He doesn't turn out the class of stuff people swallow in chunks.

THRUPP. Pity.

LORNA. It's as much as we can do to make both ends meet, not to mention the potatoes. Ha, ha! Excuse an old joke. And we've two kids who suffer terribly from foot-and-mouth disease——

THRUPP. Heavy on their shoe-leather——?

LORNA. And with enormous appetites. Their school-bills, too! Horrible facers! Have *you* any children?

THRUPP. Three.

LORNA. Where are they at this moment, may I ask?

THRUPP. Broadstairs, with the wife.

LORNA. Exactly; while my Brian and Betty are kicking their heels in that frowsy Regent's Park. The ornamental water is their sea, ill-fated little imps; we can't afford to give *them* a whiff of the briny. [*Starting up and walking to the window.*] Oh, it's shocking! It always makes my inside feel icy cold, to think of it!

THRUPP. [*Uneasily.*] I'm sure I've no wish to be unpleasant, Mrs. Gillbanks. If I'd nobody to consider but myself I wouldn't press you. But there's my partner—the property's *his,* or we might have had to distrain months ago——

LORNA. [*Coming forward on the left—dryly.*] M'yes, you have a partner—Mr. Jorkins——

THRUPP. Jorkins? No; Odlum.

LORNA. A quotation—" David Copperfield."

THRUPP. One of your husband's books?

LORNA. No, another fellow's. Party of the name of Dickens.

THRUPP. Ah, I've heard of *him.* Dead, isn't he?

LORNA. There is a rumour to that effect.

THRUPP. [*Suspecting she is quizzing him and getting to his feet.*] Bar chaff, Mrs. Gillbanks; what am I to tell Mr. Odlum?

LORNA. Tell him, with my love, that I'm jolly well certain nothing would induce him to sell us up and bundle me and my brats into the street. He couldn't

THRUPP. Yes, but that isn't business, dear lady——

LORNA. Wait; I haven't done. Listen. My husband will soon be through with the new book he's engaged on, if you don't drive him crazy meanwhile, and then he gets an advance from his publishers. I promise you faithfully Jorkins shall have a bit.

THRUPP. Oh, well, that's talking.

LORNA. [*Sarcastically.*] Yes, it isn't hopping, or skipping, or playing the trombone, is it?

THRUPP. Oh, don't be nasty; there's no occasion to be nasty. Now, when you say a *bit*——?

LORNA. Half; at least half. Anything—anything to keep Jorkins's leaky roof over our heads!

THRUPP. *Half* being—? I should like an idea of the amount, if you've no objection——

[*Colin Maccabe, coming from the right, has appeared in the front-garden and now peeps in at the open window. He is a simple-mannered, guileless-looking little man of three-and-thirty, very seedily dressed and much in need of a shave. He wears a greasy black stock of the affectedly "arty" kind and a rust-eaten sombrero hat, and carries an oil-painting—a portrait of Kit-cat size—framed in a narrow, roughly constructed frame of stained wood. The portrait is not seen, as he is holding it close to his legs. Hearing the crunching of the gravel, Lorna turns to the window.*

LORNA. [*Calling to Colin.*] Hallo, neighbour! What cheer!

COLIN. Beg pardon. I'm in the way.

LORNA. Rubbish! Come in at once. [*Colin enters, hat in hand. She introduces him to Thrupp.*] Mr.

122

Maccabe—the artist—an old friend of ours—[*presenting Thrupp to Colin*] Mr. Thrupp——

COLIN. [*Taken aback at encountering Thrupp.*] Oh, —er—Mr. Thrupp and I know each other. [*To Thrupp.*] Er—how d'ye do?

THRUPP. [*Scowling.*] How d'do?

COLIN. [*Nervously.*] I'm afraid I—I'm afraid I'm slightly behindhand with my—er—with my rent, Mr. Thrupp——

THRUPP. A good deal behindhand, Mr. Maccabe.

LORNA. [*Highly amused.*] Colin——!

COLIN. [*To Lorna.*] Hey——?

LORNA. [*Sitting on the music-stool and rocking with laughter.*] Ha, ha, ha, ha——!

COLIN. What——?

LORNA. Ho, ho, ho! We're all in this! [*To Colin.*] Don't fret. Mr. Thrupp and Mr. Jorkins are the best natured creatures in the world.

COLIN. Jorkins——?

THRUPP. [*Huffishly.*] Look heah, Mrs. Gill-banks——!

LORNA. [*To Colin.*] How many quarters are *you* in arrear?

COLIN. Two at Michaelmas.

LORNA. A trifle. We'll be three.

COLIN. [*To Thrupp.*] The fact is I've had to spend such a lot of money on the roof of my studio——

LORNA. Does it leak?

COLIN. Leak! Sometimes my sitters have to put up their umbrellas.

LORNA. That's nothing. I could bathe my children in the torrents that pour from *my* roof.

THRUPP. [*Rather disconcerted—looking at his watch and edging towards the door.*] Well, I—phiou!—by George, I must be off!

LORNA. Must you? [*Jumping up and going to him.*] Thank you so much for calling, dear Mr. Thrupp——

THRUPP. [*To Colin—opening the door.*] Good day.

COLIN. [*Throwing his hat on the round table.*] Bye-bye.

LORNA. [*Following Thrupp into the passage, where he is seen to take his hat and stick from the hat-stand.*] You won't forget to give Mr. Jorkins my fond message, will you?

THRUPP. [*Disappearing.*] Oh, drop it, Mrs. Gill-banks! 'Pon my soul——!

LORNA. [*Also out of sight.*] Ah, don't be nasty; there's no occasion to be nasty.

THRUPP. [*The sound of his voice dying away.*] I'll lay your proposition before Mr. Odlum; I can't guarantee the result——

> [*There is silence. Colin has carefully placed his picture in an upright position on the settee and is now almost dancing before it with pride. The portrait is a competently painted but conventional one of Lorna. Presently she bounds back into the room and shuts the door.*

LORNA. What a boob I am! It quite slipped my memory that you pay your rent through Odlum and Thrupp.

COLIN. Or *don't* pay it. [*Dragging her by the arm to the settee.*] Blow the rent! Come and squint! [*Pointing to the picture.*] I've finished you, Lorna. The best I've ever done of you.

LORNA. [*Standing shoulder to shoulder with him as they view the picture—after a short pause.*] Jiminy, but that's ripping!

COLIN. You like it; you really like it?

LORNA. Rather! It's *awfully* clever.

COLIN. So glad; [*putting his arm gently round her waist*] so glad.

> [*Just as gently, but firmly, she removes his arm and walks to the arm-chair on the right where she seats herself. He remains rapt in admiration of the portrait.*

LORNA. Congrats, Colin, dear boy; I congratulate you sincerely.

COLIN. I can say it to *you*, Lorna—Millais never did anything better. No, nor even Reynolds, or Gainsborough, or Romney, or Raeburn—the biggest of 'em all. [*Snapping his fingers.*] As for Shannon and Sargent—! [*Turning to her with a mournful grin.*] But it's the last; absolutely the last.

LORNA. The last?

COLIN. My swan-song.

LORNA. Bosh!

COLIN. In this style of Art. I've made up my mind, after much wrestling. I'm going in for the Primitive, the naïve—Giotto and that sort of thing, with a dash of El Greco.

LORNA. Colin!

COLIN. [*Extravagantly.*] Yes, henceforth faulty drawing is the game—distorted limbs and features, raw colour and rotten perspective. [*Strutting about.*] Behold! I'm a Primitive! Naïveté, my girl! The word is sweet in the mouth; it tastes of toffee. Naïveté! Naïveté!

LORNA. Do you believe you can create a stir that way, Colin?

COLIN. Can't fail, in these days. If I can only force myself to draw and paint badly enough I shall sell like hot cakes. [*Going to her—humbly.*] You see, Lorna, I've been wretchedly out of luck lately. Precious few commissions, paltry as my price is, and no trade with the dealers. I've got to earn bread-and-cheese somehow. D'ye blame me?

LORNA. Not I. Blame you! My stars! don't I wish Tony could be brought to change *his* style of work!

COLIN. Oh, *he's* hopeless; a sickening spectacle. [*Grinding his teeth.*] The sight of Anthony slaving and sweating year after year at the manufacture of his indigestible stodge——!

LORNA. Ah, don't be hard on him——!

COLIN. I will be hard; I *will* be. [*Leaving her and pacing the room angrily.*] Great Scott! It's all mighty fine for a writer to be content with a miserable circulation when the whole of his responsibilities are under the brim of his hat; but for a chap with a wife and young family—! [*Finding himself at the bookcase.*] Look!

Look at his row of magnum opuses up to date—[*opening the bookcase*] just read the titles——!

LORNA. [*Rising and moving towards the piano.*] Don't! don't! [*Putting her hands to her ears.*] I can't bear it.

COLIN. [*Taking some books from a shelf one by one and reading the title-pages.*] "Social and Economic History of the Middle Ages——"

LORNA. [*Trying to hush him.*] Oh, la, la; la, la!

COLIN. "By Anthony Gillbanks——"

LORNA. [*Hearing in spite of herself.*] The economic history of *my* middle age will be an interesting subject.

COLIN. "By Anthony Gillbanks, Author of Women in the Time of the Cæsars."

LORNA. Ha, ha! Why the devil didn't *I* live in the time of the Cæsars!

COLIN. [*Reading another title-page.*] "History of the Alchemists and the Rosicrucian Mysteries."

LORNA. [*Who has seated herself at the piano—opening it and running her hands over the keys.*] Be quiet, I tell you!

COLIN. [*Reading.*] "Life of Christina of Sweden, With a glance at the Military Activities of Gustavus Adolphus."

LORNA. [*Humming while she strums.*] Ral-lal de-da; ral-lal de-da——!

COLIN. [*Almost shouting another title at her.*] "The Ancient Provinces of Spain: An Attempt to Locate the Abandoned Towns and Dried Watercourses."

LORNA. You brute! [*Over her shoulder.*] Imitate the watercourses; dry up!

[*He replaces the volume he is handling and closes the bookcase; then, with a thoughtful air, he crosses over to her and touches her arm. She is now playing a simple melody softly and expressively.*

COLIN. Lorna——

LORNA. Well?

COLIN. You remember when you were in Oxford Street—the Times Book Club?

LORNA. [*Half-absorbed in her playing.*] Golly! haven't I reason to!

COLIN. [*Wistfully.*] Ah, yes, when Tony and I were both in love with you, eh—[*sighing*] rivals?

LORNA. What a couple of spoonies you were, exchanging your books regularly every day and never reading them!

COLIN. For the sake of a word or a nod from you!

LORNA. [*In tone with the music.*] Ha, ha, ha——!

COLIN. Lord! the agonies I suffered because you presided over the letter "G" and I had to go to another desk for "M"!

LORNA. Miss Dolby's desk.

COLIN. A plain wench, with an austere manner.

LORNA. Why these reminiscences, Colin?

COLIN. I'm thinking: you recollect how the women subscribers used to clamour for what you young ladies called Hot Stuff?

LORNA. They do still, I fancy, heaps of them; won't read anything else.

COLIN. [*Knitting his brows.*] Lorna, I wonder whether, if we tackled him when he's in an amiable mood, we could persuade Tony to have a shy—for mental relaxation, we could put it—we could persuade Tony to have a shy at a work of Fiction?

LORNA. Fiction? [*She stops playing and twists herself round to stare at him.*] You don't suggest——?

COLIN. [*Nodding.*] Hot Stuff.

> [*There is a moment's pause, and then she gets up and walks to the other side of the room, waving her arms and laughing to the point of hysteria.*

LORNA. Hot Stuff! Ha, ha, ha, ha! Ho, ho, ho! *Anthony!* My husband! Hot Stuff! Oh, Colin, you fool! Ha, ha, ha, ha——"

> [*He is looking after her, surprised at her outburst, when Brian and Betty straggle into the front-garden and come to the window. Spying Colin, they dash into the room and make for him. Brian is a sturdy boy of ten, Betty a spare slip of a girl a year younger. They are cheaply but neatly dressed in clothes that have been well patched and darned.*

BRIAN. Uncle Colin!

BETTY. Uncle Colin!

BRIAN. [*Seizing Colin by his jacket.*] Uncle, uncle, uncle!

COLIN. Hallo, Brian, my boy! Aha! don't tear me to pieces! [*Disengaging himself from Brian, to whom*

129

*he administers a smack on his behind, and catching hold of Betty.*] Betty! [*Lifting her up and kissing her.*] How's my sweetheart?

BRIAN. [*Going to Lorna.*] Betty got her feet wet, mother, at the lake.

LORNA. Take your cap off, Brian, and don't tell tales.

BETTY. [*To Lorna.*] Yes, and Brian was spoken to by the Keeper.

BRIAN. [*To Betty.*] Not more than you were!

LORNA. [*Smoothing Brian's hair.*] Silence! Silence!

BETTY. [*Discovering the portrait.*] Oh! A picture! Brian——!

BRIAN. Picture—? [*Turning.*] Oh-h-h-h!

BETTY. [*Flopping down on her knees before the portrait and resting her elbows on the settee.*] Have you done it, Uncle Colin?

BRIAN. Course he has, silly.

COLIN. [*Moving to the back of the settee.*] Certainly; the deed is mine.

BRIAN. I guess! [*Kneeling beside Betty.*] It's meant for mother.

COLIN. *Meant* for mother!

LORNA. Brian!

BRIAN. Aren't you frightfully tired of painting mother, Uncle Colin?

COLIN. Neither frightfully nor otherwise.

BETTY. [*To Brian.*] Painting pictures isn't tiring, stupid boy.

BRIAN. There's two of her in the dining-room, and one in father's study——

LORNA. [*Joining Colin behind the settee.*] There *are* two in the dining-room, Brian——

BETTY. Not *there's* two.

BRIAN. [*To Colin, critically.*] I say, though! Mother isn't nearly as beautiful as you've made her; not by miles.

BETTY. Yes, she is!

BRIAN. She isn't!

BETTY. She is!

BRIAN. Don't tell horrid lies. [*To Lorna.*] Mother, Betty mustn't tell lies, must she?

LORNA. [*Quietly.*] I'm afraid your brother's right, Betty. [*Sitting at the writing-table and clearing up a litter of papers.*] Uncle Colin sees me with the bloom on, as I was when he first knew me.

BRIAN. [*Fingering the surface of the portrait.*] T'any rate, she hasn't got such a nice frock as you've dressed her up in, Uncle Colin.

BETTY. T'isn't any nicer than her pink with the ribbon bows; is it, mother?

COLIN. [*Constrainedly.*] Ha, ha, ha! [*To Brian.*] Oh, that's artistic license, Brian.

BRIAN. [*Puzzled.*] Artistic—license——?

BETTY. [*Feeling the frame of the picture.*] Oughtn't it to have a gold frame—a wide gold frame with pretty blobs on it?

BRIAN. Hold your tongue! Gold frames are expensive. [*To Colin.*] You can't afford to buy a gold frame, can you, Uncle Colin?

LORNA. Gurrrh—! [*Jumping up.*] Away with you,

you—you demons! [*Stamping her foot.*] Do you hear me! [*The children scramble up in a hurry and march to the door.*] Go and wash your hands and tidy yourselves.

BRIAN. [*Obediently.*] Yes, mother.

LORNA. Change your shoes and stockings, Betty, and hang your stockings inside-out on the window-sill.

BETTY. Yes, mother.

BRIAN. [*To Colin, who has opened the door for them.*] Stay to lunch, Uncle Colin; do stay to lunch.

BETTY. Oh, yes, do, do, do, do!

BRIAN. There's roast goose to-day and apple sauce——

BETTY. And treacle tart and port wine.

LORNA. Betty! Brian! You wicked little fibbers! How dare you!

BRIAN. [*As Betty scampers away.*] All right, mother —artistic license.

[*He follows his sister and Colin closes the door.*

COLIN. [*Chuckling.*] Ha, ha, ha, ha——!

LORNA. [*Ruefully.*] I'm dreadfully sorry, Colin; we've only liver and bacon for lunch and a tapioca pudding.

COLIN. Ho, ho, ho! Ho, ho—! [*Checking himself suddenly.*] Lorna——!

LORNA. Yes?

COLIN. [*Going to her with an altered expression.*] Oh, my dear Lorna! I've a splendid notion!

LORNA. What about?

132

COLIN. Mental relaxation for Tony, and profit into the bargain! [*Bringing his hands together sharply.*] There's a fortune in it, done properly. Why the deuce hasn't it occurred to us before!

LORNA. Hasn't *what* occurred?

COLIN. The children!

LORNA. The children?

COLIN. [*His eyes sparkling with excitement.*] A book about the children. If we could manage to coax him into giving history a rest and doing a book about those urchins——!

LORNA. Brian and Betty?

COLIN. Brian and Betty. Books about children are in fashion; and take my tip, they'll be a positive rage before they're played out.

LORNA. Yes, but Tony! *Tony!* Tony write a child's book!

COLIN. You don't understand. Not a book dealing with giants and witches and old-fashioned bunk of that kind, but a record—an intimate record—of the dawning intelligence, the quaint imaginings, of the small folk; a book that analyses them, probes them, drills holes, as it were, in their baby flesh——

LORNA. [*Wincing.*] Oh, don't be so surgical in your illustrations!

COLIN. Drills holes in 'em and peers into their innocent souls. A mixture of poetry, philosophy, fun and frolic; literary entertainment for grown-ups *and* young people! [*Again pacing the room.*] My sacred aunt, what a chance for Anthony, with Brian and Betty on the spot for his models! Hot cakes again, Lorna! Hot cakes! Hot cakes!

LORNA. [*Perching herself musingly on the left-hand arm of the settee.*] Colin——

COLIN. Hot cakes!

LORNA. D'ye know, I often doubt whether Tony's fully aware of his children's existence!

COLIN. That's no disadvantage. The freshness of the material should inspire him.

LORNA. To turn his offspring into pounds, shillings, and pence!

COLIN. [*Coming to her on her right.*] Why not, if it enables the little ragamuffins to attain their ideal?

LORNA. Their ideal——?

COLIN. Roast goose and apple sauce!

LORNA. Ha, ha! Treacle tart and port wine!

COLIN. And provides 'em with warm togs in the winter and a scamper on the sands in the summer!

LORNA. [*Catching his enthusiasm and slipping from the arm of the settee.*] Oh, my gracious! [*Walking about.*] Oh, Colin you're a marvel!

COLIN. [*Preening himself.*] Well, without vanity——

LORNA. Who's to broach the scheme to him?

COLIN. [*Weakening.*] Who—who's to—broach the scheme—to him——?

LORNA. You or I, or both together?

COLIN. W-wouldn't it come better from you alone?

LORNA. [*Halting.*] Coward! Backslider!

COLIN. [*Sticking his chest out.*] Not in the least.

LORNA. [*Resuming her walk.*] Glad I'm mistaken.

COLIN. It seems to me that, in a matter concerning her children, the *wife*—the-the-the-the mother——

LORNA. I should have thought that a friendly—what's the blessed thing—intermediary——

COLIN. Afterwards. *Afterwards,* if my opinion is solicited—if I am asked to give my views——

LORNA. [*Witheringly.*] Yes, you could drop us a line, couldn't you!

COLIN. [*Pained.*] Lorna——!

[*The door is slowly opened and Anthony wanders in, smoking a pipe—a pallid, wild-haired man of five-and-thirty with a furrowed brow and rather a feeble mouth. He is wearing workaday clothes which are in a worse condition than that of mere shabbiness—his trousers in particular being grotesquely "kneed"—and his feet are partly in and partly out of a pair of broken-down slippers. Colin and Lorna are obviously discomposed by his entrance.*

ANTHONY. [*After gazing at Colin for a moment vacantly.*] Oh, you!

COLIN. Er-good morning.

ANTHONY. [*Pushing the door to.*] Wasting your time as usual, Colin—vaporizing?

COLIN. [*Annoyed.*] I *beg* your pardon——!

LORNA. [*Going to Anthony.*] You—you've knocked off early this morning, Tony.

ANTHONY. [*In a weary voice.*] Yes. Another snag! I've struck another snag.

LORNA. [*Sympathetically.*] Oh, my dear!

**135**                                                    K

ANTHONY. What's happening to me! That anything connected with the sixteenth century should land me in a difficulty! Absurd! [*Seeing the picture and advancing.*] What on earth's this?

COLIN. [*Stiffly.*] A little effort of mine.

ANTHONY. [*With conviction.*] A portrait.

COLIN. A portrait. Intelligent of you to perceive it isn't an impression of Stonehenge by Moonlight.

ANTHONY. Portrait of a woman.

COLIN. Yes; *not* of the Lord Mayor or one of the Sheriffs.

ANTHONY. [*Inquiringly.*] Lorna?

COLIN. [*Bowing.*] Mrs. Anthony Gillbanks.

ANTHONY. Is it like her?

COLIN. Oh, no, no; but the resemblance to the proprietress of the banana stall in the Finchley road is remarkable.

ANTHONY. Never serious, Colin! [*Looking at Lorna and then again at the painting.*] Yes, I suppose there *is* a likeness.

COLIN. [*Under his breath.*] P'shah——!

[*Fuming, he transfers the picture from the settee to the chair at the writing-table.*

ANTHONY. [*Promptly sinking on to the settee.*] Thanks, old man.

LORNA. [*At the arm-chair on the right, with a resolute face.*] Tony——

ANTHONY. H'm?

LORNA. News for you; Thrupp has been here this morning.

ANTHONY. Thrupp——?

LORNA. The house-agent.

ANTHONY. Ah, yes; the house-agent—agreeable fellow—Harding and Thrupp——

LORNA. Odlum and Thrupp——

ANTHONY. Is he very well?

LORNA. Very well indeed; but they demand the rent.

ANTHONY. [*Vaguely.*] The rent?

LORNA. The rent of this mansion.

ANTHONY. [*Closing his eyes.*] The beasts! The hellish beasts!

LORNA. There'll be three quarters due at Michaelmas.

ANTHONY. Michaelmas——?

LORNA. Next month.

ANTHONY. Vampires! Bloodsuckers! Tormenting me! Torturing me!

COLIN. [*Behind the round table.*] And me. I'm in arrear with my rent, too.

ANTHONY. *You,* yes! But for a man in the thick of a stupendous task—up to his neck in it——!

LORNA. [*Seating herself.*] They'll hold off for a while. I've promised 'em half what you get from Luxmore and Crowther when the job's finished.

ANTHONY. [*Horrified.*] Half! [*Drooping.*] My God!

LORNA. [*To Colin.*] Take his pipe away. He'll set the happy home on fire——

[*Colin snatches Anthony's pipe from his unresisting hand, treads out some fallen sparks, and lays the pipe on an ash-tray which is on the round table.*

ANTHONY. [*Faintly.*] Do they—do they know how much half *is?*

LORNA. No.

ANTHONY. [*Rallying.*] Ha, ha, ha! When they find out! A sublime revenge on the scoundrels!

LORNA. [*Pointing to the arm-chair by the round table.*] Take the weight off your legs, Colin. [*Colin sits, glancing at Lorna somewhat apprehensively. She clears her throat for action.*] Ah'm! Ah'mm! Colin and I were talking affairs over when you came in just now, Tony dear.

ANTHONY. Affairs——?

LORNA. Our affairs. Pretty desperate, aren't they?

ANTHONY. Extremely—[*drawing himself erect and including Colin in a lofty look*] though I am not conscious of their being appreciably worse than they've been for many years past.

LORNA. [*Ironically.*] No, it's a shame perhaps to disturb the even tenor of our alleged lives. Still, one does thirst for novelty occasionally.

ANTHONY. [*At sea.*] I don't——

LORNA. [*Plucking at her skirt and watching Colin out of the corner of her eye.*] Tony—Colin—Colin has an idea—[*ignoring a fierce glare from Colin*] a magnificent idea——

ANTHONY. [*With a supercilious smile.*] Colin——?

LORNA. For varying the monotony. Varying the monotony and incidentally producing the nimble ninepence. [*To Colin.*] Haven't you, Colin?

COLIN. [*Wriggling in his chair.*] I—er—I certainly have ventured——

ANTHONY. Really! Ha, ha! I'm curious to hear—ha, ha!——

LORNA. Order, Order! Mr. Maccabe is addressing the meeting.

COLIN. [*Pulling himself together.*] My idea is this, Tony—shortly——

ANTHONY. Oh, please don't allow your desire for brevity——

LORNA. Ssh, ssh! Sit down in front!

COLIN. My idea is this. Putting your present scale of earnings aside——

LORNA. That's all we *can* put aside—the scale!

ANTHONY. [*Frowning at her.*] Lorna——

COLIN. Putting your present scale of earnings aside, it's evident that a brain like yours must have—must have—[*to Lorna, in distress*] what was the word I used when we——?

LORNA. Relaxation, you old gumps.

COLIN. Relaxation. Intellects such as yours can't be kept on the stretch constantly without—without——

LORNA. Deteriorating——

COLIN. Without deteriorating. [*Dabbing his face with his handkerchief.*] Well, the plan I propose is that, as soon as you're free of the book you're grinding at, you should go in for an entirely different class of work; a class of work which would—which would—[*rising and retreating to the window*] it's exceedingly warm in here——

LORNA. [*Peremptorily.*] Come back!

COLIN. [*Returning, on the left.*] Exceedingly warm.

ANTHONY. [*Blinking.*] An entirely—different—class of work——?

LORNA. A lighter sort, dear.

COLIN. The sort of thing that isn't full of snags——

LORNA. [*Also rising and, with Colin, standing over Anthony.*] That won't wear you to a thread——

COLIN. That doesn't entail endless researches——

LORNA. Grubbing through folios——

COLIN. And poring over maps——

LORNA. At that ghastly Museum.

COLIN. Confound it, in a critical situation, a man is more than justified, however high his ambitions, in—in—in——!

LORNA. Adapting himself to circumstances.

COLIN. Quite so. Take my case, for example——

LORNA. Yes, take Colin's case——

ANTHONY. [*To Colin.*] *Your* case——?

COLIN. I am about to change *my* style of Art—my mode of expression——

ANTHONY. [*Repeating his disdainful smile.*] Oh, *you!*

COLIN. [*Losing his temper.*] Don't keep on saying "*you*" in that contemptuous tone, Anthony. I resent it.

ANTHONY. [*Formally.*] I apologise.

COLIN. I resent it very strongly.

LORNA. Colin——!

COLIN. Very strongly.

LORNA. Anthony has apologised——

COLIN. [*Flinging himself on to the music-stool.*] Ha! Easy to apologise——!

ANTHONY. Ssh, ssh, ssh! [*Clasping his temples.*] To prevent a vulgar wrangle, may I presume to inquire— with the utmost politeness—to what depth of abject triviality you wish me to descend, both of you?

LORNA. [*Sitting again in the arm-chair by the round table.*] A children's book, Tony dear.

ANTHONY. [*Aghast.*] A chil——!

COLIN. [*Sullenly.*] Not necessarily a trivial book, by any means.

LORNA. A *modern* book about children. They're all the vogue. No witches and pumpkins, no beanstalks— [*to Colin*] don't be sulky, Colin; tell him——

COLIN. [*Still nursing his wrongs.*] Tsch!

LORNA. A record—er—an intimate record—[*her memory failing*] oh, Colin, you *might*——!

COLIN. An intimate record of the—er—[*with a shrug*] I forget.

LORNA. [*Remembering.*] An intimate record of the dawning intelligence—the—er—the quaint imaginings of the kiddies—that's it!—[*to Anthony*] our kiddies——

ANTHONY. Our——!

LORNA. Of course. Dear little Brian and Betty are to be the hot cakes——

COLIN. No, no; the models—the models——!

LORNA. The models that make the book that bakes the hot cakes.

ANTHONY. [*Resignedly.*] Are you mad, Lorna?

LORNA. A book that analyses our children—er—

probes them to the core—eh, Colin?—drills holes in them——

COLIN. [*His enthusiasm reviving.*] Metaphorically —drills holes in their baby flesh and—and—and—and——

LORNA. And peers into the recesses of their clean, white souls.

COLIN. A blend—er—a blend of poetry, philosophy, fun and frolic; literature for the adult as well as for the youngsters. [*Pointing a finger at Anthony.*] You needn't sniff, Gillbanks. Some of our cleverest authors are at it—Cooper Davis—Hugh Wilkins—J. S. Laffiner. It's a veritable Tom Tiddler's Ground—a gold mine——

LORNA. [*Singing.*] " We're on Tom Tiddler's Ground, picking up gold and silver—"! [*Clapping her hands.*] Tony——!

ANTHONY. [*Rousing himself.*] But—but—but—but —my dear Lorna—my dear, doubtless well-intentioned Colin—granting, for argument's sake, that my brain is crying out for rest—moaning from fatigue——

LORNA. Your poor overtaxed brain——!

ANTHONY. And that my income, under the most favourable conditions, is lean to a degree——

LORNA. A mouldy skeleton!

ANTHONY. I am scarcely equipped—[*with a noble gesture*] oh, I recognise my limitations—I am scarcely equipped for twittering about children. [*Rising.*] True —as you remind me—I have two of my own——

COLIN. Charming little beggars!

LORNA. Cherubs!

ANTHONY. Possibly; possibly. A busy man hasn't much opportunity for observing the special qualities of his bantlings, attractive or the reverse. [*Roving about the room as he orates, stopping now and then to point his remarks.*] As for children in general, I admit—I frankly admit—I have no great affection for them. They are nuisances.

LORNA. [*Reproachfully.*] Tony——!

ANTHONY. To me, intolerable nuisances. Far too much fuss is made over children in the present day, too much adulation lavished on them. They are exalted to a pitch distinctly humiliating to their elders. Ha! I prefer to restrict my acquaintance with them to their pictorial appearances in the advertisements of nourishing foods. [*Halting before Colin.*] Heavens above! if I were to write such a book as you describe I should have to pose as a child-worshipper!

COLIN. Isn't all art more or less a pose? Hugh Wilkins—his books about children make people cry, they're so soppy; but I've heard he's a holy terror at home—scowls at his kids whenever they come within a dozen yards of him.

ANTHONY. [*Showing signs of wavering.*] Another consideration! [*Moving to the arm-chair on the right and sitting.*] Even if I were prepared to entertain the idea, the question arises: have I the peculiar gifts, inferior though they are, that a writer of fanciful books should possess, to be successful with the public?

LORNA. I bet you have! [*To Colin.*] He has; hasn't he, Colin?

COLIN. [*To Anthony.*] You underrate your powers, old chap. Your versatility is amazing.

ANTHONY. [*Biting his nails.*] The requisite flimsiness of touch—could I command it?

LORNA. Yes!

COLIN. Yes!

ANTHONY. And the humour? I've plenty of humour, but isn't it too pungent for the purpose, too caustic?

LORNA. [*Rising and throwing her arm round him.*] Don't let that bother you, dearest. Brian and Betty would supply the humour.

COLIN. [*Jumping up and joining them.*] I tell you what, Tony! Gird your loins! Steal an hour from your regular work every day—make a start on the thing——!

LORNA. Yes, yes; oh, yes!

COLIN. And in the evenings, after supper, I'll stroll round and listen to the stuff, and give you the benefit of my advice.

ANTHONY. [*Raising his head.*] Your——?

COLIN. [*Unsuspectingly.*] Criticise it—keep you on the right tack.

ANTHONY. [*Curling his lip.*] You, Colin! Ha, ha, ha, ha——!

COLIN. [*Recoiling.*] Anthony——!

LORNA. Oh, Tony——!

ANTHONY. [*Testily.*] There, there; I apologise, I apologise.

COLIN. You—you—you—you can apologise till you're blue in the face. [*Stalking to the farther side of the round table and grabbing at his hat.*] I've had enough of your rudeness.

LORNA. [*Hurrying after him and trying to wrest his hat from him.*] Colin! Colin——!

COLIN. No, no; no, no! [*Gaining possession of his hat and ramming it on his head.*] Good-bye, Lorna. Love to Betty and Brian.

LORNA. [*Catching his sleeve.*] Colin! Ah, Colin, don't be shirty! [*As he releases himself.*] Stop and share our liver and bacon. I insist!

COLIN. [*Bouncing out at the open window.*] Not if I never eat liver and bacon again for the rest of my life.

LORNA. [*Calling after him.*] Tapioca pudding!

COLIN. [*In the distance.*] No, thank you.

LORNA. [*Still louder.*] *My* make, Colin! M-m-my——!

> [*There is a pause, and then she leaves the window and, with tears in her eyes, seats herself disconsolately on the settee.*

ANTHONY. T'sha! We shall see him again before the week's out, my dear, never fear, and as perky and self-assertive as ever. But what a vile temper! *What* a temper! [*She snivels and, failing to find a handkerchief, wipes her eyes with the back of her hand.*] Tsch, tsch, tsch! How *can* you, Lorna! Preposterous fellow! *He* will hear me read my " stuff " and advise me upon it; *he'll* criticise my work and keep me to the right path! [*Rising and walking to the other side of the room and there striding up and down.*] Ho! I'll show our old friend Maccabe that I can write a child's book without his assistance. I'll show him that I need no guidance from him, or from any other individual!

LORNA. [*Open-mouthed.*] Tony——!

ANTHONY. Upon my word, what next!

LORNA. You—you mean to—you mean to do it?

ANTHONY. [*Facing her.*] Do it! Of course I mean to do it!

LORNA. Oh——!

[*She is on her feet when the door is thrown wide-open and Brian swaggers in noisily with Betty at his heels. Seeing Anthony, the children give a gasp and turn tail.*

LORNA. Wait! Don't go, my pets. Shut the door, Betty.

BETTY. [*Shutting the door.*] Y-y-yes, mother.

BRIAN. [*Timorously.*] Beg your pardon, father. We didn't know you were here; did we, Betty?

BETTY. No, or Brian wouldn't have made such a disgraceful clatter.

LORNA. [*Waving them away.*] Ssh, ssh, ssh!

[*The children tiptoe to the window and huddle together, eyeing Anthony loweringly.*

LORNA. [*First assuring herself that the children are out of hearing—to Anthony, in a whisper.*] Have a talk with them while I'm getting lunch ready. [*Hoarsely.*] Break the ice.

ANTHONY. The ice——?

LORNA. Be affectionate. Gain their confidence. Tell

146

'em about the book. [*Nudging him.*] Your models! Your models!

ANTHONY. [*In a flurry.*] Ah, yes, yes!

LORNA. [*Tripping to the door.*] Father wishes to have a little chat with you, Brian; and you, Betty darling.

BRIAN. [*His eyes bolting.*] With *us!*

BETTY. [*Clutching Brian.*] Oh, mother——!

LORNA. [*Merrily.*] Ha, ha, ha, ha! [*She opens the door a little way, squeezes herself through the narrow aperture, and then, with a roguish look, pops her head into the room.*] Prepare for a surprise, you ruffians; father's going to make your hair curl! [*Disappearing.*] Ha, ha, ha——!

> [*She closes the door. After a short silence, Anthony straightens himself and moves to the settee.*

ANTHONY. [*At a loss.*] Er—come here, Brian; come here, Betty. [*The children advance shrinkingly as he seats himself.*] Sit down. [*Both the children make for the chair farthest from the settee.*] No, no; why hustle each other? You sit there, Betty; [*pointing to the chair by the round table*] you here, my boy.

> [*The children sit as directed in dismay. Again there is a pause, and then Anthony suddenly beams upon them with a smile that is meant to be ingratiating but is not unlike the grin of a hyena.*

BETTY. [*Quiveringly.*] Oh——!

BRIAN. [*Breathing hard.*] We—we haven't done anything, father!

ANTHONY. [*Discouraged.*] Done anything, Brian?

BRIAN. Anything wrong.

BETTY. 'Cept bursting in just now.

BRIAN. Very well behaved during the holidays we've been, Betty and me.

ANTHONY. Betty and *I*.

BRIAN. Her and I.

ANTHONY. [*Groaning.*] Oh-h-h-h!

BETTY. [*Her mouth twitching.*] Yes, I'm sure our behaviour's been admiral—on the ole.

ANTHONY. [*Clenching his hands.*] Whole! Whole! On the whole!

BRIAN. [*Turning upon Betty savagely.*] There's a naitch in it, you idiot!

BETTY. [*Trying to repress a sob.*] I—I—I know there is, but it wouldn't sound.

ANTHONY. [*Hastily.*] Never mind, never mind, never mind. [*Already exhausted—tossing his hair back.*] Phu! [*Steadying himself.*] Er—h'm—attend, children.

BRIAN. Yes, father.

ANTHONY. Don't kick the chair, Brian——

BRIAN. No, father.

ANTHONY. And kindly refrain from snuffling, Betty.

BETTY. [*With a gulp.*] Y-y-yes, father.

ANTHONY. What I have to tell you is that, mainly to gratify your mother, I am projecting the writing of a book—er—you are aware that my profession is that of an author, children—[*getting no response*] eh?

BRIAN. [*Looking down his nose.*] Rather!

ANTHONY. [*Raising his eyebrows.*] I don't know exactly what "rather" is intended to convey, Brian.

BRIAN. [*Biting his lip.*] Beg pardon.

BETTY. [*Innocently.*] When the milkman came for his money the other day he called you a blighted scribbler, father.

ANTHONY. Oh, *did* he! I am obliged for the information. [*With a wave of the hand.*] Anyhow, with our milkman's permission, I am contemplating the writing of a book having for its theme the period of artless juvenility—your present stage of existence, children.

BRIAN. [*Finding himself addressed.*] Is it, father?

ANTHONY. [*Irritably.*] Is it! At what stage do you *think* you are, my boy? [*Brian squirms.*] You're dumb!

BRIAN. [*Gazing at the carpet sheepishly.*] Childhood's fleeting hour.

ANTHONY. Precisely.

BRIAN. [*Looking up, highly satisfied with himself.*] Learnt that at school, father.

ANTHONY. I am glad you've learnt *something* at school.

BETTY. [*Not to be outdone—spouting.*] "I thank the goodness and the grace Which on my birth have smiled,——"

ANTHONY. Ssh, ssh, ssh——!

BETTY. "And made me, in these Christian days,——"

ANTHONY. That'll do; that'll do!

BETTY. "A happy Christian child."

ANTHONY. Be quiet!

BRIAN. [*To Betty, enviously.*] Showing off!

BETTY. No, I ain't.

BRIAN. Yes, you are; you're vainglorious.

ANTHONY. Peace, peace, peace! [*Passing his hand across his perspiring forehead.*] To resume! [*With an effort.*] My dear—er—my dear little chickabiddies— [*the children prick up their ears and exchange wondering glances*] my dear little chickabiddies—in view of this approaching undertaking of mine, I conceive it to be essential that we should drop the veil of reserve which has hitherto, in a measure, obscured me from you, and establish relations of a warmer, more familiar, character. You follow me?

BETTY. B-B-Brian does, father.

ANTHONY. [*Not noticing Brian's angry glare at Betty.*] Come! Shall we make a beginning, hey? [*Repeating his dreadful grin.*] Sit beside me. [*Patting the settee.*] Boykins—girlie-wirlie—! [*The children go to him with dragging steps and he places them beside him, Betty on his right, Brian on his left.*] Now—er—I want to impress on you—don't fidget—I want to impress on you that you are to be the protagonists of my new book—[*slipping an arm round them, to their great distaste*] a distinction which I trust you'll always be proud of——

BRIAN. Wotjer mean, father—protaglists——?

ANTHONY. My chief personages—my hero and heroine.

BRIAN. [*Brightening.*] Me the hero!

ANTHONY. In a sense, the hero.

BRIAN. [*Brandishing an imaginary sword.*] Oooo—!

BETTY. And me the Princess?

BRIAN. Do I fight people, father, and slay them?

BETTY. Am I rescued from a slimy dragoon?

BRIAN. Dragon—not dragoon!

BETTY. Am I, father?

ANTHONY. [*Coldly.*] You certainly are *not,* in any work of my composition.

BRIAN. Book about kids, you said——

BETTY. Artful juvenility——

ANTHONY. *Artless* juvenility——

BRIAN. Well, then——!

ANTHONY. [*Withdrawing his arms from the children.*] A book dealing with children, yes; but a study in the manner of to-day—a book of minute observation, searching analysis.

BRIAN. [*Wagging his tongue in disgust.*] Owh——!

ANTHONY. No ridiculous adventures, no witches, no pumpkins, no beanstalks; nothing so mischievous and perversive.

BETTY. [*Despondently.*] No gurnomes?

ANTHONY. Gurnomes—? Gnomes! No, *no* gnomes, [*Rising and again pacing the room.*] I have been discussing my scheme with your mother. [*Recalling the words of Colin and Lorna.*] A record—an intimate record of the dawning intelligence of youth—its quaint imaginings—its ingenuous reactions to the problems of life——!

BRIAN. [*Chipping in.*] Shall we have to read it, father?

ANTHONY. [*Halting.*] I am really utterly indifferent as to whether you read it or not, sir.

BRIAN. [*Chastened.*] Sorry.

ANTHONY. [*Resuming his walk and losing himself in his subject.*] I warn you—I warn you, children—you will have to submit patiently, during the progress of my work, to the process of being probed—the expression is your mother's——

BRIAN. Probed!

ANTHONY. Probed to the core, you and Betty—to the core!

BETTY. To our cores!

ANTHONY. Yes, it will be necessary to probe you deeply—drill holes in your baby flesh—[*Betty and Brian, with set faces, slide off the settee, she clinging to him*] drill holes in your baby flesh and peer into your souls' innermost recesses. In addition to that——

BRIAN. [*Holding Betty tightly.*] Father——

ANTHONY. [*Between the settee and the door—pulling himself up.*] Eh?

BRIAN. [*In a level voice.*] You're not speaking the truth. Mother's never given you leave.

ANTHONY. Never given me——?

BRIAN. Leave to drill holes in us. She wouldn't let you do such a di-bolical thing.

ANTHONY. [*Moving to the children quickly.*] My dear boy and girl—! [*With a half-stifled shriek, the children flee to the window and stand there quaking.*] Dolts! Dunces! You're interpreting my words literally——!

[*The door opens and Lorna skips in, in high spirits.*

LORNA. Lunch, lunch, lunch——!

ANTHONY. [*Ruffling his hair.*] Oh-h-h-h——!

LORNA. [*Looking from him to the children.*] What's the matter? What's the matter?

ANTHONY. [*Distractedly.*] Calm your children, Lorna! Calm your children! In mercy's name——!

[*He goes out, pulling the door after him with a bang.*

LORNA. [*To the children, who run to her.*] Brian! Betty——!

BETTY. [*Clinging to her skirt.*] Oh, mother——!

BRIAN. [*Stoutly.*] Mother——

LORNA. Yes, yes? What is it, Brian?

BRIAN. Father's off his nut.

LORNA. Brian, for shame!

BETTY. He *is,* mother. He says he's going to probe us.

BRIAN. And drill holes in us and peer in.

BETTY. And he's been talking in a funny way——

BRIAN. Once or twice he nearly laughed!

LORNA. [*Sitting on the settee and drawing the children to her.*] Oh, my darlings! My treasures! Mother's bonnie bairns. [*Gaily.*] Ha, ha, ha, ha! Father's made a muddle of it. Just like him, frightening you out of your wits! We're going to be lucky, children, all of us; lucky!

BRIAN. [*Bewildered.*] Why, mother?

LORNA. Why, why, why? Because we've found Tom Tiddler's Ground—[*Colin reappears in the front-gar-*

*den and peeps into the room timidly.*] Tom Tiddler's Ground, where the gold and silver is——!

BETTY. [*Catching sight of Colin.*] Uncle Colin——!

BRIAN. Here's Uncle Colin again!

LORNA. [*Over her shoulder.*] Colin! [*Putting the children from her and rising, as Colin enters and comes forward.*] Hallo, you old sinner!

COLIN. [*Meekly.*] I—I accept Anthony's apology, Lorna.

LORNA. [*Her eyes twinkling.*] Liver and bacon?

COLIN. [*Hanging his head.*] Liver and bacon.

LORNA. So glad. [*Giving him her hands.*] Oh, Colin, it's all right!

COLIN. All right——?

LORNA. He'll do it! Tony'll do it!

COLIN. Will he!

LORNA. [*Embracing him violently.*] Bless you! Bless you! Bless you! Ha, ha, ha—! [*Singing.*] "We're on Tom Tiddler's Ground—"! [*To Brian and Betty.*] Sing, children!

[*She seizes the children, who are agape with astonishment, and, followed by Colin, prances with them round the settee.*

ALL. [*Singing.*] "We're on Tom Tiddler's Ground, picking up gold and silver——"!

END OF THE FIRST ACT

# THE SECOND ACT

*The garden of a picturesque, old-fashioned, " detached "
London villa. On the left is the back of the house.
Two French windows, sheltered by a verandah,
open into the drawing-room, and at the farther
side of the house there is a narrow gravel path
leading, it may be supposed, from the front of the
house to the tradesmen's door and thence to the
garden. Beyond the path, which continues its
course round the garden, a brick wall about eight
feet high separates the garden from the grounds of
another house of a similar character, and the adjoining house is seen a short distance away, partly
hidden by trees.*

*Running along the bottom of the wall there is
a border of flowers, but the garden is mainly lawn.
On the left, near the verandah and following the
line of the house, is an artistically designed wooden
seat, and close to this seat are a small table and a
wicker chair. Another table, with a wicker chair
on either side of it and one behind it, stands on the
right of the lawn, and in the centre, not far from
the wall, there are two more chairs, also of wicker-
work. On each of the tables there are a large box
of cigarettes, a match-bowl, and an ash-tray.*

*In the adjacent garden a short ladder is placed
against the middle of the wall, the top rung of the
ladder being a few feet above the wall.*

*The light is that of a fine summer afternoon.*

[*Nutt, an elderly two-days-a-week gardener, is on
the ladder in his shirt-sleeves, the upper part
of his body being visible, trimming a climbing
plant which is growing in the next garden and
is intruding itself over the top of the wall.
Presently Irene, smartly dressed in a parlour-
maid's uniform, enters briskly from the side
of the house. She is carrying a pile of brightly
covered pillows.*

IRENE. [*Stopping for an instant to nod to Nutt.*]
Afternoon, Mr. Nutt. How're you?

NUTT. Afternoon, miss. Nice weather.

IRENE. Heavenly. [*Distributing the pillows among
the various seats.*] Ain't we lucky!

NUTT. Got a party on, haven't you?

IRENE. Mr. Gillbanks' birthday. Biggest At Home
we've ever given.

NUTT. Reely?

IRENE. Expecting a hundred at the very least.

NUTT. And 'ow old may your guv'nor be to-day, if
I'm not arskin' a rude question?

IRENE. Forty-three.

NUTT. Forty-three? Looks a bit older, I must say,
from the glarnces I've 'ad of 'im.

IRENE. Think so?

NUTT. P'raps the strain of continu'ly bendin' over a
desk, pen in 'and, ages a writin' gentleman pre-
maturely.

IRENE. Shouldn't wonder.

NUTT. Stories about children is his strong point, I see in the papers some time back.

IRENE. That's right.

NUTT. An' there was a picture of 'im, I rec'lect, surrounded by a lot o' little mites gazin' up into his face as pretty as peaches.

IRENE. [*Who has finished the disposal of the pillows —adjusting her cuffs and the frills of her apron.*] Yes, he might be a Royalty, or Lady Diana, the way they persist in photographin' him.

NUTT. [*Pointing to the house with his shears.*] Well, it on'y shows that somethin's to be made out o' children's books nowadays, doesn't it? He, he! Almost as lookerative as bein' a jobbin' gardener in the Chelsea district! He, he, he—! [*Bobbing down and vanishing.*] Your lady——

[*Lorna, now thirty-seven but scarcely changed, appears in the room at the farther window. She is somewhat startlingly, but not vulgarly, dressed in ultra-modern fashion.*

LORNA. *There* you are, Irene!

IRENE. [*At the group of chairs farthest from the house.*] I was just coming to you. [*Advancing.*] You *are* dressed early.

LORNA. Ellen's been helping me. [*Coming into the garden.*] It's nearly half-past three.

IRENE. [*Clasping her hands in ecstasy.*] Oh-h-h-h! My—word——!

LORNA. [*Smiling.*] Do I meet with your approval?

157

IRENE. Lovely! Perfectly lovely!

LORNA. Irene, those stupid caterers have sent waitresses who've never been to us before. You'd better go and talk to them.

IRENE. [*Crossing to the nearer window.*] Ha! That's Sangsters all over!

LORNA. There's a tall one with ginger hair who is more like a duchess than any duchess who's ever breathed. Let her serve the tea and the iced coffee.

IRENE. [*Tightening her lips.*] Like a duchess, is she! [*Going into the house.*] I hope she's good form.

LORNA. [*Raising her voice.*] Irene——

IRENE. Yes?

LORNA. I've a surprise for you.

IRENE. [*Returning to the verandah.*] What——?

LORNA. [*Taking a cigarette from the box on the table by the wooden seat.*] Mr. Maccabe is home.

IRENE. No!

LORNA. Rang me up from Titus Street last night. He'd just arrived.

IRENE. [*Thinking.*] Why, how long's he been away?

LORNA. Six months—painting in the South of France —place called Vence.

IRENE. Is he coming to the party?

LORNA. Of course. Be off.

IRENE. [*Disappearing.*] Well, I *shall* be glad to see him. Fancy——!

[*Lorna is lighting her cigarette when Joan mounts*

*the ladder and peers over the wall inquisi-*
*tively. She is a sallow, plainly attired, spec-*
*tacled young lady of fourteen with a lofty*
*brow from which her hair is scratched back*
*and a nose inclined to redness.*

JOAN. [*Primly.*] Excuse me——

LORNA. [*Turning.*] Hallo! Oh, how are you, Joan?

JOAN. Nutt, our gardener, says you are receiving your friends this afternoon, Mrs. Gillbanks.

LORNA. Correct.

JOAN. It's Mr. Gillbanks' birthday, I understand.

LORNA. You've got it. [*Moving nearer to the wall.*] I say! Would you care to run in for a little while? My boy and girl will look after you.

JOAN. Oh, I'm quite capable of looking after myself, thank you very much. I'm fourteen, you know. But I don't think my parents would sanction my accepting such a short invitation.

LORNA. [*Good - humouredly.*] Sorry, I'm sure. There'll be strawberries-and-cream and all sorts of cakes. Doesn't that tempt you to put pressure on the authorities?

JOAN. No, I am strictly forbidden to eat strawberries or any soft fruit, owing to a gouty tendency. Cakes too are difficult for me to assimilate.

LORNA. Then what may I have the pleasure——?

JOAN. I want to ask you whether I may be allowed to take a few snap-shots during the afternoon with my new camera.

LORNA. [*Dubiously.*] From up there?

JOAN. Please don't refuse. [*Seating herself on the top of the wall.*] You see, I am a great admirer of Mr. Gillbanks; I've read every one of his books again and again.

LORNA. [*Sitting in the left-hand chair of the two nearest the wall.*] Have you, Joanie? That's jolly of you.

JOAN. I mean those specially appealing to Youth. I have them by my bedside, as a relief from works of a more solid kind—Shaw and others.

LORNA. And which of them's your favourite, Joan?

JOAN. Oh, I adore them all equally, from " Brian Boy and Betty the Wisp " to the latest.

LORNA. " Brian and Betty Conquer the World "?

JOAN. " Brian and Betty Conquer the World." That's wonderful !

LORNA. The first—" Brian Boy and Betty the Wisp " —is *my* favourite, Joan.

JOAN. Is it?

LORNA. [*Pensively.*] When " Brian Boy and Betty the Wisp " was written my children were mere kiddies.

JOAN. Obviously.

LORNA. Now they're what's called young people. Brian is eighteen and Betty seventeen.

JOAN. Which makes Mr. Gillbanks' recent book so particularly interesting. " Brian and Betty Conquer the World "! [*Her nose in the air.*] The triumph of my generation! [*Changing her tone and her position on the wall.*] Mrs. Gillbanks——

LORNA. [*Starting out a reverie.*] Eh?

JOAN. I trust I didn't annoy Mr. Gillbanks the other day.

LORNA. Annoy him? How——?

JOAN. I was coming from my optician's in the King's Road and I met him in the Grove. I'm afraid I stared at him.

LORNA. Oh, he's accustomed to that, Joan.

JOAN. He stood still for a moment and made a face at me. It gave me an acute palpitation.

LORNA. [*Rising uneasily.*] M-m-made a face at you——?

JOAN. Squinted in a most terrifying manner and put out his tongue.

LORNA. You—you must have been mistaken, child——

JOAN. Oh, no; I noticed it was white.

LORNA. [*Walking away and getting rid of the end of her cigarette.*] H-his fun, Joanie—ha, ha!—merely his fun. He-he-he's bubbling over with fun——!

[*Colin appears at the nearer window, hatless. His hair is now of a romantic length and he has a small up-curled moustache and a Van Dyck beard, and he is finely dressed in an elaborately braided jacket, gay-coloured trousers, and a redundantly flowing necktie.*

COLIN. [*Holding out his arms to Lorna.*] Aha——!

LORNA. Colin—! [*They meet in the middle of the garden and grasp each other's hands.*] Oh, my dear Colin—! [*She glances at the wall and sees Joan discreetly retiring; then she offers her face to Colin and he kisses her warmly on both cheeks*.] My dear, dear old pal!

COLIN. I thought I'd get here before the crowd, on the chance of having a word or two with you quietly. D'ye mind?

LORNA. Mind!

COLIN. [*Surveying her admiringly as he takes off a pair of bright yellow gloves.*] Bewitching! Absolutely bewitching! Lorna, you grow more and more enchanting every year.

LORNA. [*With a grimace.*] I'm aware of it.

COLIN. [*Pocketing his gloves.*] Seriously, I've never seen you look more beautiful—never seen you look more——

LORNA. Shut up! What's your news? Has Vence produced any masterpieces?

COLIN. [*Suddenly dropping into broken English and using outlandish gestures.*] Vence! Ah, ze colour, ze purity of ze colour! At Vence, green eet is green and blue eet is blue, and peenk eet is peenk. Zere, all nature she is *chaste—immaculé*—vat is your Eenglish vord——?

LORNA. [*Sternly.*] Colin——

COLIN. Eh?

LORNA. Don't be an ass.

COLIN. [*Hurt.*] Lorna——!

LORNA. None of your stupid affectations with me; they won't wash. [*Sitting at the table farthest from the house and pointing to the box of cigarettes upon it.*] Smoke?

COLIN. [*Bowing stiffly.*] I thank you, no. [*Going to her.*] And what is *your* news, since you evince a distaste for hearing mine?

LORNA. [*Giving him her hand.*] Ah——!

COLIN. [*Raising her hand to his lips, instantly mollified.*] Most glorious of women!

LORNA. [*Withdrawing her hand.*] *My* news? [*Her face clouding.*] Bad, Colin; rotten.

COLIN. Bad?

LORNA. I haven't bothered you with letters; where's the use!

COLIN. The children——?

LORNA. Oh, they're spry enough, bless their hearts; but they're spoilt, Colin—shockingly spoilt.

COLIN. They've been that for a long while.

LORNA. They're worse now than ever; the past few months have made a vast difference. Their heads are completely turned by their popularity.

COLIN. [*Irascibly.*] P'sh——!

LORNA. Ah, it isn't their fault, poor dears. Society —Society with a big S—has begun to fuss over them. They're being petted and flattered into a state of semi-idiocy.

COLIN. The result of Anthony's latest!

LORNA. " Brian and Betty Conquer the World." Yes, that's put the lid on.

COLIN. " Brian and Betty Conquer the World "! Of all the arrant trash—of all the unmitigated flap-doodle——!

LORNA. I agree; but what the devil are we to do?

163

The public has made a hero and heroine of the children at every stage of their growth. As a business proposition, we're bound to continue the Brian and Betty series—bring their lives up to date. Don't be inconsiderate!

COLIN. [*Moving to the back of the table with rather a guilty air.*] And Anthony—[*sitting*] how's old Anthony through it all?

LORNA. "Child Man"?

COLIN. Child Man——?

LORNA. A nickname the children have given him, to describe a simple-minded creature, half man, half child, devoted to the young. [*Mirthlessly.*] Ha, ha!

COLIN. [*In the same tone.*] Ha, ha!

LORNA. [*Staring into space and drawing a deep breath.*] Colin——

COLIN. H'm?

LORNA. It isn't only the children I'm worried about. Tony—he's altered so, lately.

COLIN. Altered——?

LORNA. Become so gloomy—so moody. And he's taken to breaking out into the most violent rages.

COLIN. Rages——!

LORNA. When we're alone. Not before the children; he's afraid of *them*. Without rhyme or reason, he stamps up and down and trumpets like a mad elephant.

COLIN. Good gracious!

LORNA. I'm as nervous as a cat over this party this afternoon; but I tell him, we must return hospitality. It's our one beano this summer.

COLIN. [*Much concerned.*] My dear Lorna——

LORNA. He's sulky with the Press too; shirks being interviewed. Deliberately declines sometimes!

COLIN. Nonsense!

LORNA. And I've asked two or three pressmen to pop in by-and-by with their photographers, to catch him in the garden!

COLIN. [*Opening his eyes widely.*] *Have* you!

LORNA. I'm determined his birthday sha'n't go unnoticed. [*Rising and walking away.*] And there's another thing that's making me anxious, Colin—preying on me.

COLIN. What's that?

LORNA. Anthony has started work again!

COLIN. Why shouldn't he?

LORNA. But without consulting me—taking me into his confidence.

COLIN. [*Rising.*] Does he always——?

LORNA. Oh, my dear fool! [*He joins her.*] As if you didn't know!

COLIN. [*Lowering his voice.*] I know you helped him at the beginning——

LORNA. At the *beginning!* Ha! [*Dropping into the chair by the wooden seat*]. Oh, Colin, how on earth he'll manage entirely on his own is beyond me!

COLIN. Perhaps he's bent on showing you that he *can*.

LORNA. [*Brightening.*] He's got into a muddle, you think, and is too proud to confess it!

COLIN. Possibly.

LORNA. And it's that that's making him so damned irritable!

COLIN. [*Twitching his little moustache.*] His behaviour's atrocious, whatever the cause may be. And your old friend—your faithful old friend and lover—has to stand by and look on! [*Laying his hand caressingly on her shoulder and heaving a sigh.*] Ah, Lorna——!

LORNA. [*Eyeing his hand.*] Well?

COLIN. What a chance—*what* a chance in life we've both missed!

LORNA. [*Shaking herself free.*] Now, Colin——!

COLIN. Oh, it's no disloyalty to Anthony to say that he ought never to have married. He's totally unfit to be a married man.

LORNA. Be quiet!

COLIN. [*Leaving her side and strutting about.*] Whereas here am I at the top of my tree, able to give you every comfort, every conceivable luxury——

LORNA. [*Dryly.*] Yes, but you mustn't be as primitive in your morals as you are in your Art, Colin dear.

COLIN. [*Halting.*] Where you are concerned, I admit that my morals are distinctly loose, Lorna.

LORNA. Ssh, ssh!

COLIN. With regard to yourself, I admit that I am a potential wife-stealer. [*She jumps up.*] I am! [*Waving his arms.*] I cry it aloud from the house-tops.

LORNA. [*Stamping her foot.*] Colin——!

COLIN. I declare that if you were to come to me tomorrow—to-night—and ring my studio bell—! [*He is*

*interrupted by seeing Betty at the nearer window.*]
Ah, Betty——!

> [*Betty, in an extremely daring afternoon-party
> frock, swaggers into the garden. She is a pretty
> girl, but she has a strident voice and a pert
> manner, and is altogether thoroughly " bad
> style."*

BETTY. [*Going to Colin and giving him a finger.*]
Heard you were here, old thing. Still alive, then!

COLIN. [*Mildly.*] How are you, Betty, my darling?

BETTY. [*Looking him up and down.*] My God!
Irene ought to have prepared me. Who built that
jacket?

LORNA. Betty——!

BETTY. And those bags!

LORNA. Aren't you going to give Uncle Colin a kiss,
Betty?

BETTY. No, thanks; I'm not fond of slobbering. [*To
Brian, who now appears at the window.*] Step softly,
Brian. Ever seen anything so impressive?

> [*Brian comes into the garden. He is an effeminate
> youth with the slimmest of waists, an exposed
> throat, and finicking movements—the personi-
> fication of conceit.*

BRIAN. [*Strolling with an undulating walk to Colin
and shaking hands with him languidly.*] Hail to thee,
deah lad!

COLIN. [*Biting his lip.*] How do you do, my boy?

LORNA. [*At the nearer window.*] Where's Child
Man, Brian?

167                                                    M

BRIAN. [*Shutting his eyes and shuddering.*] Don't ask me, Lorna.  He is producing in me a feeling of positive nausea.

LORNA. Brian——!

BETTY. [*Flaunting about at the back.*] And me. We're sick at the stomach.

LORNA. Betty——!

BRIAN. An undeniable fact, mother mine.  Child Man has been exceptionally tahsome to-day.

BETTY. Dam nuisance, in my opinion.

LORNA. For shame, both of you! [*Disappearing into the house.*] I'll rout him out.

BRIAN. [*Putting an arm round Colin.*] Your luscious work; how goes it?  Tell me, O Master! are we to be staggered—are we to be struck all of a heap by the fruits of your labours down South?

COLIN. [*Wriggling out of Brian's embrace.*] Thank you, I am very much obliged to you for inquiring——

BETTY. [*Practising the steps of a dance as she speaks.*] Yes, I expect you've got acres of new jazz to show us at the studio, haven't you, Colin?

COLIN. Jazz——!

BRIAN. [*Shrilly.*] Ho, ho, ho! [*Squatting on the ground in a girlish way.*] Betty, you impudent little baggage!  I shall chastise you; I shall reahly.

BETTY. Plenty of highly coloured streaks and splodges, I bet!

COLIN. [*Drawing himself up.*] I certainly have returned from abroad with several important canvasses—

BRIAN. Glad tidings!

BETTY. Golly! I shall take a pair of smoked glasses with me when I view them.

COLIN. [*To Betty.*] You have not yet, I may remind you, received an invitation to view them, young lady. [*Espying Anthony, who has come through the room and is standing, half concealed, at the nearer window lowering at them all.*] Anthony——

BRIAN. [*Turning to the window.*] Oh, come on, Child Man; come on and let's have a look at you.

> [*With lagging feet and downcast eyes Anthony emerges and goes to Colin. He is a ridiculous object. His hair is plastered close to his head in boyish fashion, and his clothes, stretched tightly upon his now puffy figure, are modelled after those of Brian. As he has aged considerably beyond his years, his juvenile get-up is the more absurd.*]

ANTHONY. [*Shaking hands with Colin abjectly.*] Colin——

COLIN. [*Viewing Anthony's rig-out with some surprise.*] Congratulate you, Anthony.

ANTHONY. Congratulate me——?

COLIN. Your birthday.

ANTHONY. Oh—ah—yes.

COLIN. [*Without warmth.*] Many happy returns, and so on.

ANTHONY. Thank you.

BRIAN. [*Who has risen and is inspecting Anthony critically.*] H'm! Passable. Just passable. [*Arranging the set of Anthony's jacket.*] Ssst! The fat on your shoulder-blades is revolting. Turn round. [*Anthony shakes himself rebelliously before complying.*] Now, don't be tahsome. Oh, Child Man, will you never learn to tie a bow properly?

ANTHONY. [*As Brian re-ties the bow—grinding his teeth.*] It's the accursed butterfly effect that eludes me.

BRIAN. Steady, steady! No bad language, I beg.

BETTY. [*Still dancing.*] In the hearing of a simple maiden!

LORNA. [*Showing herself for a moment at the nearer window and then again disappearing.*] Brian—Betty—come away and leave Child Man and Uncle Colin to have a talk together.

BETTY. [*Skipping into the house at the farther window.*] Time too! My male parent is swearing like a beery dustman.

BRIAN. [*Following Lorna and Betty — over his shoulder.*] Now, don't go and get yourself untidy, Child Man. If you do, I shall be cross with you; [*out of sight*] I shall reahly.

> [*There is a pause after the two men are left alone, during which neither speaks. Then Anthony goes slowly to the chair at the left of the right-hand table and drops into it.*

ANTHONY. [*Feebly.*] Colin—[*Colin, who has wandered away to the back, comes forward.*] my children; what do you think of my children?

COLIN. [*Evasively.*] Er—oh, a remarkably handsome young couple. [*Eyeing him askance.*] You ought to be proud of 'em.

ANTHONY. [*Raising his head.*] Proud——!

COLIN. [*Gulping.*] Tremendous improvement in 'em since I was last with you; tremendous.

ANTHONY. Colin——

COLIN. In manner and appearance; striking improvement.

ANTHONY. [*With concentrated bitterness.*] I hate 'em.

COLIN. Anthony——!

ANTHONY. I hate 'em, I hate 'em, I hate 'em, I hate 'em.

COLIN. Hate them! Your own flesh and blood! Upon my word, I've never heard anything more unnatural.

ANTHONY. [*Extending his arms.*] Look! Look at me! Only look at me! D'ye see?

COLIN. See——?

ANTHONY. How they dress me up; how they insist on dressing me up.

COLIN. Well, isn't it appropriate?

ANTHONY. Appropriate——?

COLIN. To the character you bear before the world —a lover of the young from the cradle onwards; a—a— a—a Child Man.

ANTHONY. Ah—! [*Rising deliberately and going to Colin and fixing him with a fierce glare.*] Devil!

COLIN. Eh——?

ANTHONY. Devil!

COLIN. What do you mean, sir?

ANTHONY. I owe all this to you. It was you who tempted me, dastardly emissary of hell.

COLIN. How dare you address me in these terms?

ANTHONY. [*Shaking his fist in Colin's face.*] You knew—don't deny it!—you knew I had no excessive fondness for children; you knew that I chafed at their growing influence in modern life. I saw their domination coming; I've watched it spreading—spreading like a virulent disease. [*Leaving Colin and walking about.*] And I have prostituted my talent by furthering the movement! Thanks to your meddling—thanks to your besotted officiousness—I am recognised—acclaimed— as the children's apostle—their arch-priest. I of all people! Heaven forgive me, if there is a heaven that interests itself in literary affairs; heaven forgive me!

COLIN. [*Buttoning his jacket.*] Well, I don't presume even to guess what action heaven will take in the matter; but, speaking for myself, I've done with you finally. [*Marching to the nearer window.*] Good afternoon.

ANTHONY. [*Wheeling round.*] Colin——

COLIN. [*From under the verandah.*] Accept my best wishes for a highly successful party.

ANTHONY. [*Weakly.*] Don't—don't go, Colin.

COLIN. [*Lingering.*] A devil! An emissary of hell! I've never been so affronted.

ANTHONY. I—I apologise. [*Again sinking into the chair at the right-hand table.*] I apologise.

COLIN. So you ought, [*coming back into the garden*] you—you—you—you—you ungrateful fellow.

ANTHONY. Ungrateful——!

COLIN. You forget what you were eight years ago—
what we both were; the plight we were in. [*Gesturing
towards the house.*] Phaugh! Compare this charming
villa with your dilapidated abode in the Mimosa Road;
compare that reeking little studio of mine, where I
could have cultivated mushrooms on the floor-boards,
with my present quarters in Titus Street. To-day we
exude prosperity; exude it.

ANTHONY. Yes, but at what a cost; what a terrible
cost! Eight years ago, in spite of my pecuniary em-
barrassments, I had moments of complete satisfaction,
moments of supreme serenity.

COLIN. *Had* you! *I* hadn't.

ANTHONY. *You,* no!

COLIN. Gillbanks——!

ANTHONY. [*Hastily.*] I apologise; I apologise.

COLIN. Complete satisfaction! Serenity! With a
wife who was little better than a slave, and two kids
almost in rags and tatters. Selfish beggar!

ANTHONY. You make no allowances; no allowances.
A certain amount of selfishness is an attribute of the
artistic temperament.

COLIN. Artistic temperament be blowed! If I thought
for a single instant that *my* temperament——

ANTHONY. *Yours,* no—! [*As Colin is starting for
the nearer window.*] I apologise. At any rate, what am
I now! Nobody recollects my valuable contributions
to history; they're buried under a mountain of pap.
As a serious writer, I am extinct, obsolete, dead as a
salted herring. And my reward, the treatment I receive

from my family? [*Rocking himself to and fro.*] Oh, Colin—oh, my dear old friend, you can't imagine the miserable existence I lead!

COLIN. [*With a tinge of sympathy.*] Miserable——?

ANTHONY. Badgered by Lorna to keep the pot boiling, as she chastely expresses it; tyrannized over—bullied—by my son and daughter——

COLIN. Dash it, I wouldn't stand it from *them!* Why don't you put your foot down? If I were in your place, I—I'd——

ANTHONY. [*Sighing.*] Ah, if you were in my place, you—you— [*Breaking off and looking at Colin half fearfully, half cunningly.*] Colin——

COLIN. Yes?

ANTHONY. [*Beckoning to him.*] Colin— [*Clutching his arm and speaking in a low, hoarse voice.*] I can trust you with a secret?

COLIN. Secret——?

ANTHONY. [*Rising and whispering into Colin's ear.*] I—I am at work again.

COLIN. Indeed?

ANTHONY. [*Quakingly.*] Shall I—shall I tell you my subject?

COLIN. [*Slightly startled.*] Subject——?

ANTHONY. [*Holding up a finger.*] On your honour —on your honour——!

COLIN. Of course, of course, of course.

ANTHONY. Lorna would tear up my papers, and the children would assault me—I believe they'd assault me!—if they had the faintest suspicion— [*listening,*

174

*and then suddenly pushing Colin from him*] h'sh——!
[*Brian and Betty, singing in unison a popular song
from a comic opera, enter at the farther window carrying an " upright grand " gramophone which they stand
at the corner of the lawn.*] W-w-what's that? [*Louder.*]
What's that?

BRIAN. Oh, use your eyes, Child Man. Can't you
see what it is?

COLIN. Gramophone.

BETTY. Gosh! You are cute, Colin.

BRIAN. Frightfully sorry to interrupt, but we've only
just time for our rehearsal.

ANTHONY. [*Sheltering himself behind Colin.*] Rehearsal——?

BRIAN. [*Coming forward, while Betty selects a re-
cord and puts it on.*] The dance. Clarence and Gladys
Potter are taking part in it, and Harold and Ivy Crewe,
They're heah.

ANTHONY. Dance——!

BRIAN. [*Doing some steps not ungracefully.*] In
glorification of your birthday, Child Man.

BETTY. [*Coming forward.*] On the lawn at four-
thirty.

BRIAN. And at intervals afterwards.

ANTHONY. [*Hurrying Colin across to the nearer
window.*] Come—come into my room——

BRIAN. [*To Anthony.*] No, no——

BETTY. Stop——!

BRIAN. We shall want you, hero of the hour.

BETTY. Rather!

ANTHONY. [*Under the verandah.*] W-w-want *me!*

BRIAN. Yes, you're in it.

ANTHONY. In it!

BETTY. You're the star of the blooming show.

BRIAN. The idea is, at the finish we form a circle——

BETTY. And you leap into the middle——

BRIAN. And we dance round you.

BETTY. And then we all go down on our bony knees—

BRIAN. Adoringly.

BETTY. [*Posturing.*] With uplifted hands.

ANTHONY. I—I won't.

BRIAN. [*Sharply.*] What!

BETTY. [*Elevating her eyebrows.*] Hullo!

ANTHONY. I—I refuse.

BRIAN. [*Incredulously.*] You—refuse——?

BETTY. Gregory! Here's airs!

ANTHONY. I—I—I refuse to make a greater guy of myself than I am already. [*Advancing a few paces.*] Er—er—er—understand me——

BRIAN. [*To Colin, frowning.*] Colin, go and tell them—Clarence and Gladys and Ivy and Harold—that we're waiting—Betty and I and Child Man. Run along, deah lad! [*Going to Anthony as Colin, ignoring an appealing glance from Anthony, sneaks into the house.*] Look heah, Child Man——

ANTHONY. Brian, I repeat—I—I—I repeat——

BRIAN. And I repeat, you've been exceedingly tahsome to-day; more so than usual. You're vexing me and Betty almost beyond endurance.

BETTY. [*Perched on the arm of the chair on the left of the right-hand table—swinging her leg.*] Yes, you're too leprous.

BRIAN. [*To Anthony.*] You've simply got to do as you're told, Child Man——

BETTY. Simply.

BRIAN. [*To Anthony.*] There's been an inclination on your part lately to be fractious, and it has to cease; it has reahly.

BETTY. You've got to know your place, darling, and keep it.

BRIAN. That is, with *us*. Before company you may play up a bit.

BETTY. Swank to your heart's content.

BRIAN. But when we're by ourselves, understand *me*——

BETTY. No cheek.

BRIAN. No bumptiousness.

ANTHONY. [*Subsiding into the chair by the wooden seat and gasping.*] Oh! Oh! Oh, you—you—you——!

BRIAN. Now, be careful, Child Man. Don't say anything in the heat of the moment that you'll regret.

BETTY. Anything that'll set us against you.

BRIAN. Instead of whimpering and—and——

BETTY. And whining——

BRIAN. And being generally tahsome, you ought to remember what you owe to us—to Betty and me.

BETTY. By Gum, yes!

BRIAN. How we've dragged you out of obscurity——

BETTY. [*Joining Brian.*] Given you a top-hole posish in the literary world——

BRIAN. Given you something to write about——

BETTY. Our wonderful personalities.

BRIAN. But no, you're like all those of matuah age——

BETTY. *Won't* be modest and retiring.

BRIAN. *Will* expose your sores by the wayside——

BETTY. [*Looking into the house.*] Here are the laggards. [*Bounding back to the gramophone.*] Whoo-oop!

BRIAN. [*Calling.*] Oh, make haste, you people; shake a leg!

ANTHONY. [*Struggling out of his chair and stamping across to the other side of the lawn.*] Gur-r-rh!

BRIAN. [*To Anthony, in an undertone.*] Now, do throw yourself into the spirit of the thing, Child Man——

   [*Gladys and Ivy enter at the nearer window, Clarence and Harold at the farther window. They are of the same type as Betty and Brian. Gladys is carrying a large wreath of laurel, Ivy a bunch of cut flowers.*

GLADYS. [*Running to Anthony.*] Child Man!

IVY. [*Following Gladys.*] Child Man!

ANTHONY. [*Turning to them with his hyena-like grin.*] Lambkins!

GLADYS. [*Slipping the wreath over his head.*] Many happy returns of the day, Child Man.

ANTHONY. What an honour; but how naughty of you to spend your pennies on me in this way!

IVY. [*Fixing her flowers in his jacket.*] Many happy returns of the day, Child Man.

ANTHONY. You spoil me, children; you'll end by making your big boy horribly conceited.

> [*Clarence and Harold come to him, Clarence with a small book in his hand, Harold carrying a nasty little walking-cane with a tassel attached to it.*

CLARENCE. [*Giving the book to Anthony.*] My poems, Child Man.

ANTHONY. [*Reading the title.*] "Blood Drippings."

CLARENCE. [*Painfully.*] "Blood Drippings."

ANTHONY. [*Pressing the volume to his bosom.*] This means a sleepless night, Clarence. I sha'n't close my eyes till I've read every line—caught every drip.

HAROLD. [*Presenting the cane.*] Child Man——

ANTHONY. [*Admiring the cane.*] Harold——!

HAROLD. If evah I meet you walking without it, I'll cut you. I'll cut you. [*Slapping Anthony playfully.*] There!

BETTY. [*Starting the music.*] Hi, hi, hi——!

> [*The young people dance—Betty with Clarence, Brian with Ivy, Harold with Gladys.*

BRIAN. [*After a few steps.*] Oh, I say, skip the prelude; come to Child Man.

ANTHONY. [*Under his breath.*] Oh——!

BETTY. The ring! The ring!

> [*Without ceasing to dance, the dancers form a*

*ring, linking themselves together and circling round. At the same moment Lorna and Colin appear at the farther window and look on anxiously.*

BRIAN. [*To Anthony.*] Stand by, Child Man; stand by!

ANTHONY. [*Reeling,*] Eh? Eh——?

BETTY. Pull up your socks, Child Man. Ready?

BRIAN. *Now——!*

[*Steeling himself for the effort, Anthony breaks through the ring and poses in the middle of it with a benign expression. As he does so, Joan, who has again scaled the ladder in the adjoining garden, is seen with her camera.*

BETTY. [*To the dancers — suddenly.*] On your knees! On your knees!

[*The dancers flop upon their knees in a devotional attitude.*

GLADYS. Holy Smoke! I'll ruin my stockings.

IVY. Same here.

JOAN. Hold that position, please. Hold it!

BRIAN. [*To Joan.*] Good afternoon.

BETTY. Afternoon, little 'un.

ANTHONY. [*Facing Joan.*] Who are you; who are you?

JOAN. I'm the young lady next door. Don't move.

ANTHONY. Go away! Go away!

LORNA. [*Waving at Joan.*] Get down, Joanie.

BRIAN. No, no——

BETTY. Certainly not.

GLADYS. No, do let her stay.

IVY. Yes, let's be snapped.

ANTHONY. Go away!

LORNA. Joan——!

JOAN. [*To Lorna.*] I beg your pardon; you gave me permission, Mrs. Gillbanks——

ANTHONY. [*Frantically.*] Go away!

BETTY. Shut your mouth, Child Man!

LORNA. Betty——!

[*While the hubbub is at its height, the curtain falls. It rises again after a brief interval. The gramophone is playing. Some empty teacups and ice glasses and a few plates with spoons and strawberry-stalks upon them—débris of the tea-party—are on the tables and, further indicative of the lapse of time, the light is warmer, throwing different shades from those previously seen. Lady Torbrick is sitting on the wooden seat, talking to Lorna, who is in the chair near by. Anthony is seated on the other side of the lawn, his face pale and his body limp from weariness and exhaustion. He is still burdened with the laurel wreath, and the flowers remain in his button-hole, but the flowers are withered and the leaves of the wreath ragged and shrunken. Marjorie is squatting on the ground in front of him, making a drawing of him in a sketch-book. At the back Colin and Miss Plant are sitting close together in animated conversation. In a group*

*under the verandah are Brian, Betty, Gladys,*
*and Ivy. The girls are smoking. Presently*
*the group moves into the house at the farther*
*window and the music fizzles out.*

MARJORIE. [*A fashionably-dressed young woman—*
*to Anthony, whose eyelids are drooping.*] Open your
eyes, Mr. Child Man.

ANTHONY. [*Hastily rousing himself.*] Eh——?

MARJORIE. I'm just on the finishing touches.

ANTHONY. [*Resuming a set position.*] I—I beg your
pardon.

LADY TORBRICK. [*A pleasant-looking matron—glanc-*
*ing round.*] Dear me! I've outstayed nearly everybody. [*Rising.*] We must be going. Thank you, dear
Mrs. Gillbanks, for a most delightful afternoon. [*Shak-*
*ing hands with Lorna, who has risen with her.*] What
a brilliant gathering! I've enjoyed myself enormously.

LORNA. [*In a murmur.*] Glad.

LADY TORBRICK. [*Going to Marjorie.*] Marjorie——

MARJORIE. Oh, wait a sec, mother.

LADY TORBECK. Darling, remember your engage-
ments to-night. [*To Anthony, who rises.*] Congratulate you, dear Mr. Gillbanks—I suppose *I* mayn't give
you your pet name——

ANTHONY. [*With his grin.*] Oh, do.

LADY TORBRICK. Congratulate you on your birthday,
and on your adorable son and daughter. No wonder
you write such fascinating books about them. [*Shak-*
*ing hands with him.*] *Good*-bye——

ANTHONY. *Good*-bye——

LADY TORBRICK. Child Man. There, I've said it! Ha, ha, ha! [*Joining Marjorie, who has got to her feet and is showing her drawing to Lorna.*] Now, Marjorie!

MARJORIE. [*To Lorna.*] I'll polish it up at home and then, if you'll let me——

LADY TORBRICK. [*Fussily.*] Yes, yes, yes. [*To Lorna, who is moving towards the nearer window.*] No, no; don't come, Mrs. Gillbanks.

[*She bustles into the house, followed by Lorna and Marjorie.*

MARJORIE. [*To Lorna—as they disappear.*] Where are your nice boy and girl?

LORNA. We'll find them.

[*Anthony has sunk back into his chair. Gradually he falls asleep.*

MISS PLANT. [*A gushing spinster of uncertain age— to Colin, noticing Lady Torbrick's and Marjorie's departure.*] I do believe we're the very last. Tell me the time, Mr. MacNab.

COLIN. [*Who has relapsed into his broken English and is again gesticulating extravagantly—looking at his watch.*] Six heures et demi—'alf pas' seex.

MISS PLANT. [*Jumping up.*] How disgraceful of me! But it's your fault, you wicked wretch, you!

COLIN. [*Flattered.*] Ah, *cruelle; cruelle!*

MISS PLANT. I could listen for ever to your talk about Art. What's the place you've been painting at in the South of France?

COLIN. [*Rhapsodically.*] Vence—ze divine Vence—!

MISS PLANT. Where the colour is as pure as a virgin's blush, you say.

COLIN. *Exactement.* At Vence green eet is green and *jaune* eet is *jaune,* and blue eet is blue. [*Blowing a kiss to the air.*] Ah, ze *bleu de ciel!* Ze *blue de ciel!*

MISS PLANT. [*Wriggling.*] Oh, if I could only meet you by chance some day at Vence!

COLIN. Zere all nature she is *chaste—immaculée—*I forget your Eenglish vords—[*discovering that Lorna has returned and is standing at the nearer window regarding him with disfavour*] er—er——

LORNA. [*Coldly.*] Colin——!

COLIN. [*To Miss Plant—much discomposed.*] Er— in fact, Vence is an extremely jolly little town.

MISS PLANT. [*Shaking hands with Colin.*] Goodbye, dear Mr. MacNab. Such a privilege to make your acquaintance. [*Turning to Anthony, whose mouth is open and who is breathing stertorously—lowering her voice.*] Oh, poor Mr. Gillbanks! We've tired him to death. [*To Lorna.*] I won't disturb his slumbers. Forgive me for staying to this unearthly hour. [*Taking Lorna's arm.*] A perfectly gorgeous party! I've revelled in every moment of it.

LORNA. [*As before.*] Glad.

COLIN. [*Still uncomfortable under Lorna's gaze.*] Er—I—I'm off too. [*To Miss Plant.*] Can I gif you a leeft—er—can I give you a lift, dear lady?

MISS PLANT. Oh, how sweet of you! [*To Lorna.*] Isn't he an angel?

LORNA. [*Grimly.*] Well, not yet. By-and-by, per-haps——

COLIN. [*To Miss Plant.*] Where do you live?

MISS PLANT. Highgate.

COLIN. [*To himself, his jaw falling.*] Highgate!

[*Maliciously but silently Lorna laughs at him over her shoulder as she and Miss Plant go into the house. Colin stalks after them in dudgeon.*

MISS PLANT. [*Encountering Betty and Brian in the room and shaking hands with them.*] Good-bye, you two lovely young people; good-bye.

BETTY. Must you?

MISS PLANT. He, he, he! Mr. McNab is carrying me off to my humble dwelling.

BRIAN. Reahly?

MISS PLANT. Think of the distance! *Now* who says the age of chivalry is past!

LORNA. A taxi, Colin?

COLIN. [*Haughtily.*] Please.

[*Lorna, Miss Plant and Colin disappear as Brian saunters into the garden from the farther window. Attracted by Anthony's snoring, which has become deeper and more regular, he stands contemplating his parent with an evil expression. Presently Betty joins him and adds her look of repugnance to his.*

BRIAN. [*After a pause—between the snores.*] Disgusting.

BETTY. Loathsome.

BRIAN. Repellent.

BETTY. Poisonous.

BRIAN. Shall we wake him——?

BETTY. And tell him off?

BRIAN. *I* consider that his behaviour this afternoon, taking it altogether, has been most unsatisfactory.

BETTY. Foul.

BRIAN. Grossly offensive.

BETTY. Merely because the newspaper men can't remember his footling old tosh——!

BRIAN. He snubs them.

BETTY. Crinkles his nose at them.

BRIAN. Who *does* remember that he ever wrote anything before he wrote about us!

BETTY. Who!

BRIAN. Who!

> [*Betty, singing a tune at the top of her voice, catches hold of Brian abruptly and dances with him, both watching for Anthony to awake. In a little while Anthony sits up and stares at them.*

ANTHONY. B-B-Brian—B-Betty——

BRIAN. [*Pulling up.*] Yes?

BETTY. Pleasant dreams, I hope?

ANTHONY. Is it—is it over?

BRIAN. Yes, it *is* over.

BETTY. Bally well over.

ANTHONY. Has it—been a success?

BRIAN. Partially.

BETTY. Small thanks to you, if you'll allow me to pass the remark.

ANTHONY. I'm sure I've done my utmost to—to—to —to contribute——

BRIAN. You've done your utmost to put the newspapers off us.

BETTY. To get their shirts properly out.

BRIAN. Your treatment of the pressmen was abominable.

BETTY. *And* the photographers.

BRIAN. Devastating.

BETTY. You made my spine curl horribly.

BRIAN. Once or twice I broke into quite a perspiration.

BETTY. So did I; I had beads on the brow.

ANTHONY. [*With an attempt at loftiness.*] I—I—I— I trust I was not guilty of any deliberate rudeness; of any—er——

BRIAN. You were as curt as a policeman on his beat.

BETTY. Beyond kicking their shins, I don't know what else you could have done to rub them all up the wrong way.

BRIAN. A more deplorable lack of cordiality I've nevah witnessed.

BETTY. Speaking plainly, you've gone and disgraced yourself.

BRIAN. Tahsome isn't the word.

ANTHONY. Your—your—your—your mother had no right to spring this herd of journalists and camera-men upon me; she had no right——

BETTY. Go on; pitch into Lorna!

ANTHONY. [*Holding his head.*] Oh! Oh——!

BRIAN. Yes, attack Lorna.

BETTY. I wouldn't be cowardly as well as bad mannered if I were you.

BRIAN. [*Walking away.*] Phaugh!

BETTY. [*Walking away in another direction.*] Phuh!

ANTHONY. [*Clenching his hands.*] And for this—this—I have sacrificed a day's work; for this blasted party!

BRIAN. Silence!

BETTY. [*Returning to Anthony.*] I agree — this blasted party——!

BRIAN. [*Rejoining her.*] You—you unutterably vulgah man!

BETTY. [*To Anthony.*] And if the party is blasted, who has blasted it, pray?

BRIAN. And while we're on the subject, what *is* the work you're pretending to be so busy about?

BETTY. Yes, you're mighty mysterious over it.

BRIAN. You haven't read a syllable of it yet to Lorna; not a syllable.

BETTY. Nor to Brian and me.

BRIAN. What aspect of our characters—Betty's and mine—are you proposing to deal with in your next book, may we venture to inquiah?

BETTY. You may be wasting your time, you know.

BRIAN. Certainly; we may not approve of the scheme.

BETTY. It may be a what-d'ye-call-it—an abortive effort.

BRIAN. Not worth the paper it's written on.

BETTY. Getting above yourself, it strikes me!

BRIAN. Swollen headed.

BETTY. Outgrowing your chapeau.

BRIAN. I'm not shaw that you don't deserve to be reduced to the miserable condition we rescued you from; reahly I'm not.

BETTY. Great Solomon! A pretty pickle you'd be in if we refused to let you write about us any more.

BRIAN. [*Pushing Betty aside and standing over Anthony.*] And we *shall,* you know, if you continue to be tahsome.

BETTY. *That* we shall.

BRIAN. As we've reminded you before to-day, you ought to go down on your knees to us.

BETTY. And grovel.

BRIAN. Kiss the hems of our garments.

BETTY. Basking in our thingummybob—our refulgence!

[*Lorna appears at the nearer window with a scared face.*

LORNA. Tony——

BETTY. [*To Lorna.*] Hullo?

LORNA. [*Advancing.*] I want Child Man. [*To Anthony.*] Tony——

[*Anthony, who has shrunk into his chair, crushed by the onslaught upon him, raises his head and looks at Lorna glassily.*

ANTHONY. What——?

LORNA. I—I'm dreadfully sorry. He apologises for being late. He—he has been detained——

ANTHONY. [*With a dry throat.*] Who—who apologises——?

BRIAN. For being late?

BETTY. Who's been detained?

LORNA. [*To Brian and Betty.*] A young gentleman the *Magnet* has sent to interview Child Man—[*referring to a card she is twisting in her fingers.*] Mr. Berkeley Shrimpton. [*Uttering a guttural sound, Anthony collects himself and rises.*] Oh, but he's *such* a dear, Anthony. He's having a cocktail in the dining-room. [*To Brian and Betty.*] Go and look after him, children.

BETTY. [*Moving to the verandah and there waiting for Brian.*] Right'o!

BRIAN. [*To Lorna.*] We've just been scolding Child Man for his standoffishness with the Press—reprimanding him seveahly. [*Following Betty.*] *You'd* bettah have a talk to him, Lorna——

LORNA. [*Laying a beseeching hand on Anthony's arm.*] Anthony—Anthony——!

> [*Betty and Brian are about to enter the house when Berkeley Shrimpton presents himself at the nearer window.*]

BETTY. Here *is* Mr. Simpson.

SHRIMPTON. [*Airily.*] Shrimpton.

BRIAN. [*To Shrimpton.*] How do you do?

BETTY. [*Offering her hand to Shrimpton, who comes to her.*] I'm Betty, formerly Betty the Wisp.

SHRIMPTON. [*A lively, debonair, boyish young man, not a day more than three-and-twenty—shaking Betty's hand warmly.*] Happy to meet Betty.

BRIAN. I'm Brian.

SHRIMPTON. [*Shaking hands with Brian.*] And Brian.

LORNA. [*Introducing Anthony.*] M - m - my husband——

SHRIMPTON. [*Going to Anthony and wringing his hand.*] Ha! Child Man! Excuse the impertinence, but we've heard of your nickname. How *are* you?

ANTHONY. [*With icy, studied politeness, but with an ominous glint in his eyes.*] Thank you, I——

SHRIMPTON. [*Rattling on without a pause.*] Awfully grieved to be so late; I've had an appalling rush to-day. I promise not to keep you long. My photographer will be here in a minute or two. [*Lorna and Brian have hurriedly dragged a chair forward and placed it near Anthony.*] Oh, thank you very much; too kind of you. [*To Anthony.*] Shall we sit down?

ANTHONY. [*Obviously repressing his feelings.*] By all means.

SHRIMPTON. [*As they sit.*] My method of interviewing isn't the ordinary one, you'll be relieved to hear. I'm an Impressionist, *I* am; an Impressionist.

ANTHONY. An Imp——?

SHRIMPTON. Impressionist. I don't put a string of questions. I simply say, "tell me about yourself," and lean back and listen as though I'm listening to the humming of bees. Ha, ha, ha, ha! Forgive the comparison. When the buzz slackens I say, " tell me *more* about yourself"; and when it ceases altogether I run away and paint my picture. The picture may be true or false, but it expresses my individuality; it does express my individuality. [*Settling himself in his chair and crossing his legs.*] Tell me about yourself.

ANTHONY. [*Moistening his lips.*] *Your* individuality——?

LORNA. [*Who, full of apprehension, has seated herself behind the table by the two men—to Shrimpton, hastily.*] Er—my husband has had rather a fatiguing afternoon, Mr. Shrimpton, and I—I'm afraid——

ANTHONY. [*Hushing her with a gesture.*] No, no; not in the least.

BRIAN. [*Standing close to Betty, both sharing Lorna's fear of an explosion.*] Yes, you have, deah Child Man.

BETTY. Yes, you have, belovéd.

BRIAN. Why shouldn't Mr. Shrimpton interview *us* instead of Child Man—Betty and me?

BETTY. Great stuff, yes!

ANTHONY. No, no; no, no. [*To Shrimpton, formidably.*] You are very young, Mr. Shrimpton.

SHRIMPTON. Oh, very, very. I'm accused of being ridiculously young; but I've already written a couple of books of reminiscences, and I've another on the stocks.

ANTHONY. Reminiscences——?

SHRIMPTON. Oh, there's a great deal to be made out of what happened last week. Why wait till it occurred fifty years ago? [*Settling himself again and half closing his eyes.*]  But don't bother about me. Tell me about yourself.

[*Irene appears at the nearer window.*

IRENE. [*Announcing.*]  Miss Vancuff.

LORNA. *Who?*

IRENE. *Something* like Vancuff.

LORNA. [*Rising.*]  I don't know anybody of that name——

SHRIMPTON. [*Bestirring himself.*]  Yes, yes; that's all right. Van Koff—Miss Van Koff. A young American lady who's over here doing celebrities for Tallentyre's Magazine. Biggest circulation of any magazine in the United States. I met her this afternoon at her Embassy. May she join us? [*To Irene.*]  Bring her into the garden, will you? [*Irene vanishes.*]  Pardon the liberty; [*to Lorna, who is creeping across to Brian and Betty*] I was sure you wouldn't mind receiving her. [*Patting Anthony's knee.*]  Fine advertisement for your little tales; and you're killing two birds with one stone.

ANTHONY. [*On the point of choking.*]  I—I—I—I——

SHRIMPTON. Oh, don't say you've no use for advertisement. Everybody begins by saying that, especially those who are out for it. [*Gaily.*]  Ha, ha, ha! I always tell people, advertisement is one of the oldest and therefore one of the most respectable institutions. We read of it in the Bible—in Holy Writ. I admit it originated with Satan—when the Serpent appeared to Eve and said, " Eat More Fruit "——

[*Irene shows Miss Van Koff into the garden and withdraws.*

MISS VAN KOFF. [*A sparkling little woman of five-and-thirty, speaking with a pronounced but pleasant American accent—to Lorna, who holds out her hand.*] Well, this is sweet of you, Mrs. Gillbanks—you are Mrs. Gillbanks, aren't you?

LORNA. [*Faintly.*] Yes.

MISS VAN KOFF. Allowing me to besiege you like this! [*Seeing Betty and Brian.*] Are these your celebrated children?

LORNA. [*With a gulp.*] Yes.

BETTY. Yes, I'm Betty.

MISS VAN KOFF. Betty the Wisp! [*Shaking hands vigorously, first with Betty, then with Brian.*] And is this Brian?

BRIAN. [*Archly.*] Brian Boy.

MISS VAN KOFF. Well, I'm just thrilled to meet you both; that I am. [*Going to Shrimpton and Anthony, who have risen.*] Mr. Shrimpton, it's perfectly heavenly of you, procuring me this honour. [*To Anthony.*] Mr. Gillbanks—? [*Taking Anthony's hand and pressing it to her heart while Shrimpton moves to the back of the table near Anthony.*] I'm just thr-r-r-rilled—I'm just thrilled to meet the famous Child Man.

SHRIMPTON. [*To Anthony.*] Shall we sit down?

ANTHONY. [*Dropping into his chair helplessly.*] B-b-by all means.

SHRIMPTON. [*Sitting at the table in his easy attitude.*] Now! Tell us—tell us about yourself.

MISS VAN KOFF. [*Sitting in the chair vacated by Shrimpton.*] Why, yes, tell us what gave you the urge to depict the wonderful operations of the youthful mind. Had you ever employed your pen previously, Mr. Gillbanks, or was it your first es*say* in literature?

ANTHONY. M-m-madam——!

[*Lorna sinks on to the wooden seat and Brian and Betty walk away quickly to the edge of the lawn.*

LORNA. [*In a weak voice.*] Oh! Oh, Miss Van Koff——!

MISS VAN KOFF. [*Turning to her.*] My! I guess I've said something very stupid.

LORNA. My husband is the author of several important books of an historical and social character——

ANTHONY. Ha——! [*Losing the last vestige of self-control and leaping to his feet.*] Yah! Ya-a-a-ah——!

LORNA. Anthony! Anthony——!

BRIAN. Child Man——!

BETTY. Darling!

ANTHONY. [*Trampling up and down the lawn wildly.*] Employed my pen previously! Employed my pen previously! [*Stopping to hiss at Miss Van Koff.*] H'sss——!

MISS VAN KOFF. [*Shrinking.*] Oh——!

ANTHONY. Yes, I had employed my pen previously, and to a noble purpose until I misused it by exploiting these—these—these detestable children of mine.

LORNA. [*Rising.*] Tony——!

[*Miss Van Koff and Shrimpton also rise and Betty and Brian come to Lorna.*

ANTHONY. Will you give me a puff, Miss Van Koff; will you give me a puff, Mr. Shrimpton?

MISS VAN KOFF. Why, c-c-certainly.

SHRIMPTON. [*Joining Miss Van Koff.*] Y-y-yes, tell us m-m-more about yourself.

ANTHONY. [*Halting again.*] Paragraph that I've done with babbling about children—done with babbling about children, and that I've resumed my studies in history.

LORNA. [*Clinging to Betty.*] My husband isn't well, Miss Van Koff.

BETTY. Frightfully seedy.

BRIAN. Nervous breakdown.

ANTHONY. And please announce the title of my next work—a work which is at present absorbing all my thought, all my energy.

MISS VAN KOFF. [*Diplomatically.*] Oh, but that's fine! The title——?

SHRIMPTON. Title——?

ANTHONY. "A New Light on Queen Elizabeth."

[*Lorna, Betty, and Brian gently fall against one another.*

LORNA. [*Groaning.*] Oh-h-h-h!

MISS VAN KOFF. "A New Light——"?

SHRIMPTON. "On Queen Elizabeth"?

ANTHONY. I—I hope for a Spring publication. Meanwhile, I—I beg you will excuse me from saying anything further. [*Putting his hand to his forehead.*] Good afternoon, madam; good afternoon, Mr. Shrimpton.

[*He turns from them and sits, almost in a state of collapse, in the remaining chair at the back. After a moment's pause, Miss Van Koff and Shrimpton tiptoe towards the nearer window.*

MISS VAN KOFF. [*To Anthony, as she passes him—under her breath.*] Good afternoon.

SHRIMPTON. [*In the same way.*] Good afternoon.

MISS VAN KOFF. [*Shaking hands with Brian and Betty.*] Good afternoon.

BRIAN. Good afternoon.

BETTY. Good afternoon.

MISS VAN KOFF. [*While Shrimpton is shaking hands with the young people—to Lorna, who is at the window.*] Don't stir; I guess we can find the street.

LORNA. [*Unsteadily.*] No, no——

[*Miss Van Koff and Shrimpton follow Lorna into the house, and then, after a quick look at the receding figures, Betty and Brian make a dash at Anthony and stand over him vindictively.*

BRIAN. Gur--r-r-rh——!

BETTY. Ugh-h-h-h!

BRIAN. So this is what you're up to, is it!

BETTY. This is what you've been locking yourself up in your study for, for weeks!

BRIAN. Why you've been hiding your nasty dirty papers!

BETTY. Sneak! Sneak!

BRIAN. Hypocrite! Treacherous hypocrite!

BETTY. Eating your food with us every day, and drinking your Vichy, with this on your conscience!

BRIAN. Meals we earn for you!

BETTY. By the sweats of our brows, as it were!

BRIAN. [*Walking about.*] Oh——!

BETTY. [*Walking about.*] Oh——!

BRIAN. Detestable children, are we! Ho, ho, ho, ho!

BETTY. Detestable! Ha, ha, ha!

BRIAN. Reptile!

BETTY. Scorpion!

BRIAN. *We* detestable!

BETTY. *We!*

BRIAN. [*Returning with Betty to Anthony.*] Admired for our attractive qualities, not only by the public——

BETTY. Wherever we go.

BRIAN. By people of refainement——

BETTY. Discerning friends.

BRIAN. [*His voice rising to a squeak.*] Speak! Speak!

BETTY. Speak! [*Stamping.*] Say something!

[*Lorna enters with a rush.*

LORNA. [*Distraught.*] Oh! Oh-h-h-h——!

BRIAN. [*Going to her.*] Lorna——!

BETTY. [*Going to her.*] Lorna——!

LORNA. [*Embracing them.*] Oh, my dears! Oh, my pets!

BRIAN. [*Releasing himself.*] Ha, ha, ha! Splendid opportunity for Mr. Shrimpton to do a spicy article about us, what!

LORNA. Magnificent!

BETTY. And Miss Van Koff!

BRIAN. For American consumption!

BETTY. I see it! "Former Fond Father Fouls Own Nest"!

BRIAN. [*Pointing to Anthony.*] Go for him, Lorna.

BETTY. [*Pushing her towards Anthony.*] *We've* begun.

LORNA. [*Seizing Anthony by the coat-collar and shaking him.*] Anthony! Anthony! You're mad!

BETTY. Dotty!

BRIAN. Raving lunatic!

LORNA. You're ruining us; you'll bring us all to want again—beggary.

BETTY. We shall be paupers at this rate.

BRIAN. Nice prospect!

LORNA. [*Beside herself.*] Tony! [*Hitting him upon the shoulder.*] Tony——!

ANTHONY. [*Lifting his head.*] Ah! [*Getting to his feet.*] Ah——!

LORNA. Listen to *me*——

ANTHONY. [*Seeing red.*] To you! I curse the hour I ever listened to you—to you and your vulgar, greedy ambitions. Out of my sight, woman!

LORNA. [*Gripping his arm.*] Anthony——!

ANTHONY. [*Shaking her off so that she stumbles against the table near to her.*] Out of my sight! [*To Betty and Brian, who advance to him threateningly.*] And you! Out of my sight! Monsters! Monsters of my creating! Monsters in human form! Abnormalities!

LORNA. [*Sinking into the chair behind the table, wailing.*] Oh! Oh! Oh——!

[*Betty and Brian hurry to her.*

BETTY. [*To Anthony.*] Pig!

BRIAN. [*To Anthony.*] Hog!

LORNA. B-b-brute! Brute!

ANTHONY. [*Discovering that he is still decked in the*

199

*laurel wreath.*] Tscha-a-a! [*Tearing off the wreath and flinging it at his wife and children.*] Tscha-a-a-a——!

    [*Once more Joan, camera in hand, mounts the ladder in the adjoining garden and looks over the wall.*

JOAN. [*To Anthony.*] Pardon me for intruding again——

ANTHONY. [*Recoiling.*] Hey——!

LORNA. Joan——!

JOAN. I find I made a wrong exposure——

ANTHONY. [*Catching up one of the pillows and hurling it at her.*] You red-nosed little beast!

    [*Joan drops her camera and falls off the ladder with a screech as Irene enters at the nearer window preceding Mr. Ince and his assistant, the former carrying a large camera in a case, the latter a tripod.*

IRENE. [*Allowing the men to pass her.*] Mr. Ince.

ANTHONY. [*To Ince.*] Who are you? What are you?

INCE. [*As his assistant is planting the tripod.*] Mr. Shrimpton's photographer, sir.

ANTHONY. *Are* you! Then hell fire consume you!

    [*He upsets the tripod with a furious kick and staggers into the house. Lorna rises with a cry of horror while Irene, Betty and Brian run to pick up the tripod.*

INCE. [*To Lorna, who goes to him appealingly.*] Well, all the years I've been in this business——!

END OF THE SECOND ACT.

# THE THIRD ACT

*The scene is an artist's studio and living room—a spacious, solidly-built apartment. In the wall on the right is a door, furnished with a latch-lock, opening into the room from the landing of a common stair; and in the wall facing the spectator are two other doors. One is a little to the right of the centre, and admits to a bedroom; the other, over which hangs a portière, is not far from the left-hand wall and opens into a bathroom. In the left-hand wall, directly opposite the main door, is the fireplace, with a bell-push on either side of it. No fire is burning. A clock is on the mantelpiece.*

*On the nearer side of the main door are the electric-light switches, and at its farther side, attached to the upper part of the wall, there is a small battery and door-bell.*

*The furniture and decoration of the studio suggest prosperity. Against the right-hand wall, on the nearer side of the main door, is a richly carved Jacobean cupboard with doors at the top, drawers in the centre, and doors below; and at the farther side of the main door, also against the wall, is an oaken coffer, close to which, set obliquely towards the fireplace, is a cheval-glass. Against the back wall, between the right-hand corner of the room and the bedroom door, there is a capacious marqueterie wardrobe; between the bedroom door and the*

*door of the bathroom is a handsome settee; and be-
tween the bathroom door and the left-hand corner
of the room there is a dwarf bookcase filled with
well-bound volumes.*

*At the farther side of the mantelpiece there is
another oaken coffer, and on the nearer side stands
a writing-table with a small chair before it. A tele-
phone-instrument is on this table, and, in addition
to the usual writing materials, a box of cigarettes,
some pipes, a tin of tobacco, etc.*

*In the middle of the room there is an easel. On
it is a small unfinished landscape painted in the extreme " primitive " style. At the right of the easel
a palette, colour-tubes, and brushes are on a low
table, and on the other side of the easel is an oblong
fauteuil-stool with cabriole legs.*

*At a short distance from the easel, on the left, is
the platform of a model throne. Its ornate chair is
not on the platform, but stands beside it on its
right, and between the platform and the writing-
table is a winged arm-chair upholstered in velvet.
A pair of slippers are on the floor near this chair.*

*On the right of the room, between the easel and
the wardrobe, there is another arm-chair and,
nearer the spectator, between the easel and the
Jacobean cupboard, are a circular table and a chair
without arms.*

*The room is in some disorder. The writing-table
is littered with an accumulation of letters, bills,
circulars, etc.; on the platform there is a big port-*

*manteau, partly unpacked, with a quantity of cloth-
ing, soiled shirts, and other articles of male apparel
lying close to it; on the chest against the right-hand
wall there is a travelling-bag of medium size; and
several unframed canvasses are loosely stacked
against the bookcase, the settee, and the mantelpiece.*

*There are numerous objects of art about the
room, the pictures on the walls being mostly of the
same school as the landscape on the easel.*

*It is evening, but the daylight of " summer-time "
entering from the unseen windows in the fourth
wall of the room makes artificial light unnecessary.*

[*At the rise of the curtain there is the sound of a
key in the lock of the door opening from the
landing, and then Mrs. Lumb enters and closes
the door behind her. She is an exceedingly
plain, dumpy little woman of fifty, in severe,
if somewhat rusty, black. A bunch of keys
hangs from her waistband and she is carrying
a small suitcase and a pencilled note in an
envelope. Crossing to the other side of the
room, she stands the suitcase on the platform
of the model throne and examines the envelope
inquisitively as if longing to unstick it. Ultimately she lays it on the writing-table and,
after a prying look round, goes into the bedroom, leaving the door slightly ajar. Scarcely
has she disappeared when the turning of a key*

203

*in the lock is heard again and Colin, evidently
in a very fretful mood, limps in wearily,
dressed as when last seen. He bangs the door
to, chucks his hat and gloves on to the arm-
chair between the easel and the wardrobe and,
muttering to himself, takes off his jacket and
throws it over the chair. Then he picks up his
slippers and, sitting in the winged chair, proceeds to tug at his boot-buttons.\**]

COLIN. [*Under his breath.*] Tscha! P'sh! Phuh!
[*Mrs. Lumb re-enters, shutting the bedroom door.*]
Hallo!

MRS. LUMB. [*Sidling to him with an unctuous smile.*]
Good evening.

COLIN. [*Testily.*] Evening, Mrs. Lumb. What are
*you* up to?

MRS. LUMB. Seeing whether Edith has turned your
bed down. So forgetful, that girl is. [*Kneeling and
taking off the boot he has unbuttoned.*] Here, let
Lumby help you.

COLIN. [*Submitting with an ill grace.*] Oh, thank
you.

MRS. LUMB. [*Loosening the toe of his sock and putting his foot into a slipper.*] I'm afraid something's
erritated you. You do seem grumpy, an' no mistake.

COLIN. Yes, something *has* erritated me; annoyed me
intensely.

---

*The boots which Colin is wearing, it is almost needless to say,
are of patent-leather and have light tops and buttons of mother-of-
pearl.

MRS. LUMB. [*Unbuttoning the other boot.*] What is it? Tell Lumby.

COLIN. A dreadful person fastened on to me at a party this afternoon; literally fastened on to me.

MRS. LUMB. [*Ogling him.*] Female, of course?

COLIN. Female. Lured me on to take her home, and when we got there would lug me indoors.

MRS. LUMB. [*Coyly.*] Oh, my!

COLIN. Bored me stiff for over an hour. I could have cried. Lives at the North Pole, too! Such a cab fare!

MRS. LUMB. [*Wagging her head at him.*] Ah, you men! Dessay you encouraged her, to start with. [*Taking off the boot and loosening his sock.*] But it's the old story; d'rectly you've had enough of us you cast us aside like a used bus-ticket.

COLIN. I confess I was rather attracted by her at first——

MRS. LUMB. He, he, he! I'll be bound you were. [*Putting his foot into the other slipper.*] Reg'lar Don Juan you are; a reg'lar Don Juan.

COLIN. Nothing of the sort; nothing of the sort. [*Leaning back in his chair.*] What's the time, Mrs. Lumb?

MRS. LUMB. [*Glancing at the clock as she rises, and pressing his boots to her bosom.*] Twenty-five to nine.

COLIN. I'll put on a pair of easy shoes by-and-by and run out and get a bit of food at " The Wish-Bone."

MRS. LUMB. [*Slowly shutting an eye.*] Beg pardon; you can't go out till you've seen your visitor.

COLIN. Visitor——?

MRS. LUMB. There's been a lady after you; a nice-looking lady. Left her sootcase and a note.

COLIN. Lady——?

MRS. LUMB. Ten minutes ago. Wrote the note in my setting-room an' said she'd take a walk round the houses an' be back shortly. Quite a state of mind she was in; couldn't keep still a second.

COLIN. [*Sitting upright.*] Where——?

MRS. LUMB. [*Pointing.*] There's her note; and there's her receptacle.

COLIN. [*Rising and going to the writing-table.*] Who—? [*Picking up the envelope.*] Oh—! [*Tearing it open and reading the note.*] Heavens!

MRS. LUMB. [*Hurrying to him.*] What's the matter?

COLIN. [*Passing her and dropping on to the fauteuil-stool and reading the note again and again.*] Good Lord! Oh! Oh! Oh——!

MRS. LUMB. [*Following him and reading the note aloud over his shoulder.*] " Frightful flare-up at home since you left. Am coming to you."

COLIN. [*To himself.*] " Frightful flare-up at home ——"

MRS. LUMB. " Since you left."

COLIN. " Am coming to you."

MRS. LUMB. What's her name? " L—o—r——"

COLIN. [*Hastily screening the note.*] Mrs. Lumb! [*Rising indignantly.*] A private letter!

MRS. LUMB. Sorry, I'm sure.

COLIN. My fault, my fault, my fault.

206

MRS. LUMB. My excitement carried me away.

COLIN. [*Walking to the back in great agitation and there pacing to and fro.*] I—I—I—I confide in you, Mrs. Lumb; I confide in you.

MRS. LUMB. [*Waddling in pursuit of him.*] That's right, dearie; pour your heart out to Lumby.

COLIN. I place the fullest confidence in you; the fullest confidence.

MRS. LUMB. You may; you may safely.

COLIN. [*Advancing.*] In fact, I regard you as a friend —a friend.

MRS. LUMB. And a friend in need is a friend indeed, I always maintain.

COLIN. [*Flourishing the note.*] This is the end—or, rather, the culmination—of a romantic attachment, Mrs. Lumb; a romantic attachment.

MRS. LUMB. Gone on for a long while, has it?

COLIN. [*Sitting on the fauteuil-stool again, and again spelling out the words of the note.*] Years. What *can* have happened? Years—years.

MRS. LUMB. [*Clapping his boots together.*] Silly fool I am! Isn't that her portrait in your bedroom—on the wall by the hot an' cold?

COLIN. [*Nodding.*] It is.

MRS. LUMB. [*Standing at the round table.*] Struck me I reckonised her!

COLIN. No novel that's ever been written has a more romantic story—a more extraordinary—[*Breaking off and looking at her queerly.*] Mrs. Lumb——

MRS. LUMB. [*Eagerly.*] Yes, dearie?

COLIN. Er—I ought to mention perhaps—I ought to mention that the lady is—er—a married lady.

MRS. LUMB. Not getting on well with her husband?

COLIN. [*Gnawing his fingers.*] An impossible man; absolutely an impossible man.

MRS. LUMB. Pore soul! I see it all. I might be at the cinema. [*Smirking.*] But married or single——!

COLIN. Quite so; doesn't make much difference, does it?

MRS. LUMB. He, he, he! None, to my mind.

COLIN. And I can rely on you to make things comfortable here for both of us—for this lady and myself—temporarily, at any rate? [*Not receiving a prompt answer.*] Eh? Eh?

MRS. LUMB. [*With a change of tone.*] Mr. Maccabe—

COLIN. W-w-what?

MRS. LUMB. [*Blandly.*] May I take a seat for 'alf a minute?

COLIN. [*A little dashed.*] Er—oh, do; do.

MRS. LUMB. [*Sitting at the table.*] And—between you an' me—may Lumby reveal her true nature?

COLIN. Your—true——?

MRS. LUMB. [*Facing him.*] Mr. Maccabe, I s'pose you consider me highly respectable?

COLIN. W-w-why, of course.

MRS. LUMB. And I am; I *am*—highly respectable. A more respectable woman than Mrs. James Lumb doesn't exist on this wide earth.

COLIN. I—I—I'm certain of it.

MRS. LUMB. Wait! [*Arranging her skirt circum-*

*spectly.*] Respectable, yes—through force of circumstances. [*Inflating her chest.*] But for preference, give me vice.

COLIN. Mrs. Lumb——!

MRS. LUMB. [*With gusto.*] I repeat, vice for me all the time.

COLIN. R-r-r-really?

MRS. LUMB. My plainness has always stood in my way. Oh, I've never deceived myself; I'm as plain as plain can be.

COLIN. [*Tactfully.*] Oh, I—I should hardly——

MRS. LUMB. 'Ush, now; no 'oneyed words. I was born plain, and I've acted accordingly. Being born plain means that you're doomed to respectability, and I've accepted my doom with Christian resignation. My late husband was verger at St. Simon's, Notting 'ill, and I had the cleaning of the vestry and the organ loft and one o' the aisles. There's respectability for you! You should hear how I'm spoken of in church circles to this day; in hushed whispers they speak of me. But, as I say, for choice give me vice. Outwardly I'm an icicle; inwardly I'm all for ardent love, and marriage bonds may go hang.

COLIN. [*Constrainedly.*] Ha, ha, ha! A-a-a-a whited sepulchre, hey?

MRS. LUMB. I don' know anything about sepulchres, white or coloured, but I do know I'm a daring puss; or should 'a been if I'd had a ghost of a chance. [*Cocking her head on one side.*] S'pect you're a trifle shocked an' surprised, ain't you?

COLIN. I—I—I am a little surprised.

MRS. LUMB. Yes, I must sound bold and brassy; but ever since I lost James I've suffered from what's called ree-action. After twenty-two years and seven months of married life with a verger, you can't wonder at a bit of ree-action, can you?

COLIN. N-no; no.

MRS. LUMB. That's why I applied for the position of housekeeper at the Beaufort studios, artistic gentlemen having a reputation for fastness. They may be frolicsome an' free-mannered as a rule; but my doom follers me even to Titus Street. The gents at the Beaufort studios are as respectable as the vicar an' the curates at St. Simon's.

COLIN. They *are* a sober, steady lot.

MRS. LUMB. 'Orrerbly disappointing. [*Leaning forward.*] Confidence for confidence, Mr. Maccabe; when I first came here I went so far, in sheer desperation, as to offer myself to Mr. Wagstaff—[*glancing skyward*] Studio Number Four—as a model for the figure. Thank you, Geneviève, he said—my name being Lily, mark you—thank you, Geneviève; try the College of Surgeons.

COLIN. Very rude of him.

MRS. LUMB. [*Gloomily.*] I own I did take it in the light of a rebuff; but I oughtn't to have rebelled against my doom.

COLIN. [*Rising, to end the conversation.*] Rude and unfeeling of old Waggy.

MRS. LUMB. [*Brightening.*] Anyhow, you can jest

imagine, can't you, the happiness of getting a soupsong of vice into the studios at last?

COLIN. [*Frowning.*] The term "vice," Mrs. Lumb—

MRS. LUMB. He, he, he! I could dance with joy. [*Waving Colin's boots and singing.*] "Oh, his head was in a whirl, she was sech a pretty girl, An' he cried out Ain't I luck-luck-lucky—!" [*Jumping up.*] One of George Hickley's songs——

COLIN. [*With growing impatience.*] Yes, yes, yes——

MRS. LUMB. [*Jigging.*] "An' he took her by the hand to the music of the band, An' said Come into the arbour, ducky!"

COLIN. [*Techily.*] Bravo, bravo! Capital! Excellent! [*Hurrying to the chair on which he has thrown his jacket.*] The bell'll ring in a moment——

MRS. LUMB. [*While Colin is struggling into his jacket —panting.*] S'cuse me; clean off my head I am. [*Standing the boots on the chair by the table and bustling over to the suitcase.*] That's the worst of having an excitable temperature.

COLIN. [*Feverishly adjusting his necktie at the cheval glass.*] Filthily untidy the place is. Pigsty! Perfect pigsty!

MRS. LUMB. [*Fumbling with the catches of the suit-case.*] Never mind, dearie; love rises superior to a little muck and muddle.

COLIN. Not even a flower to welcome her! There ought to be flowers. [*Pressing Lorna's note to his lips.*] The studio ought to be a mass of flowers. [*Slipping the note into his pocket.*] It ought to be a bower—a floral bower. [*Seeing that Mrs. Lumb has succeeded in opening the suitcase.*] What are you doing? What are you doing?

MRS. LUMB. [*Gloating over the contents of the suitcase.*] Careless of her. Fancy not locking it!

COLIN. [*Going to her.*] A liberty! You mustn't do that; you mustn't do that.

MRS. LUMB. [*Taking out a smart set of pyjamas.*] Oh how dainty! [*Unfolding and displaying them.*] Oh! Oh! Soft as silk!

COLIN. [*Examining them with her.*] They *are* silk; they *are* silk. [*Grabbing them.*] As though she'd wear anything but silk next to her velvety skin!

MRS. LUMB. [*Continuing her rummaging.*] If James had ever caught me wearing that kind o' night attire, there would 'a been a rumpus. [*Producing a pair of "mules."*] Gracious! Tiny feet she's got!

COLIN. [*Refolding the pyjamas clumsily.*] Put them back; put them back.

MRS. LUMB. [*Finding a sponge-bag.*] Her own sponge, too. That shows what a particular lady she is.

COLIN. Put them *back*, Mrs. Lumb. [*Together they repack the suitcase and refasten it.*] What about supper; what about supper?

MRS. LUMB. You're not going out, then?

COLIN. Certainly not. I can't take *her* to "The Wish Bone"—a rowdy club—and it's too late for the restaurants.

MRS. LUMB. There's the remains of the piece o' pickled pork you had last night.

COLIN. Pickled pork——!

MRS. LUMB. You hardly touched it. Edith an' me put it down to your having had a bad crossing.

COLIN. I *had* a bad crossing——

MRS. LUMB. Yes, I felt it was an error of judgment on my part.

COLIN. But don't you understand, Mrs. Lumb? Do, for heaven's sake, rise to the occasion! The—the—the —the crowning of a romance which has survived every obstacle—endured for half the lives of two passionately devoted people! There's no romance in cold pickled pork.

MRS. LUMB. [*Snapping her fingers.*] I got it! Stoopid o' me not to rec'lect!

COLIN. What——?

MRS. LUMB. Mr. Pollard—Studio Number Three— he's dining at the Arts to-night——

COLIN. Well, well?

MRS. LUMB. I'd cooked him a chicken before he had his invitation—he was on'y arst as a stop-gap in my opinion——

COLIN. Chicken——!

MRS. LUMB. I'll borrer it, an' explain in the morning.

COLIN. Pollard's the most amiable chap in the world——

MRS. LUMB. And I've got a lettuce that'll make you a salad.

COLIN. There's a delicacy—a refinement—about a chicken——

MRS. LUMB. Trimmed up with a sprig o' parsley.

COLIN. [*Gesturing.*] A'ha! *Le poulet froid avec la salade de laitue! C'est magnifique! C'est—!*

MRS. LUMB. An' the pork'll come in nicely with it.

COLIN. [*Grasping her hand.*] God bless you; God bless you.

MRS. LUMB. [*Admiringly.*] You *have* learnt the lingo whilst you been away, haven't you!

COLIN. Unavoidable; unavoidable. [*Pushing her towards the table.*] Lay the table; lay the table.

MRS. LUMB. That I will, dearie.

[*She scurries to the cupboard and from one of the drawers she drags out a table-cloth and spreads it on the table. Then from the upper part of the cupboard she produces knives and forks, a cruet-stand and a salt-cellar, glasses, etc., etc. While she is doing this, Colin, now in great spirits, moves about rapidly, putting the room in order.*

COLIN. [*Tidying the litter on the writing-table.*] She's such a neat woman; such a neat woman. Neatness personified.

MRS. LUMB. You'd guess as much from the way her sootcase was packed. No 'urling things in, like some ladies.

COLIN. And as beautiful as she's neat, as you've seen for yourself; as beautiful as she's neat.

MRS. LUMB. [*Smoothing the table-cloth.*] Not a stain on your table-cloth to offend her eyesight, at all events. [*Opening the upper part of the cupboard.*] I'd defy a princess to find a trace of egg or mustard on it.

COLIN. [*Gathering up the clothes, shirts, etc., from the platform and carrying them in stages to the wardrobe, where he bundles them in.*] I'll have to hit on some other place for my clothes. She'll want to hang hers here by-and-by probably.

MRS. LUMB. [*Laying the knives and forks, etc.*] Sure to. It's her due.

COLIN. [*Glancing at the oaken coffers.*] I'll clear out these chests; they'll do for me.

MRS. LUMB. And she'll insist on having the drawers in your bedroom for her linggery, you take my word for it.

COLIN. No need to insist; she'll know they're at her service.

MRS. LUMB. Any amount of frocks an' mantles she's got, I suspect?

COLIN. Oh, heaps, I should say; heaps, heaps.

MRS. LUMB. An' hats too?

COLIN. Innumerable.

MRS. LUMB. I could accommodate some of 'em downstairs, to oblige her.

COLIN. Thank you; thank you.

MRS. LUMB. Her trunks'll be coming along pretty soon, I s'pose?

COLIN. I suppose so; I suppose so. [*Shutting the portmanteau and standing it on the chest at the farther side of the fireplace.*] I shall hear the—er—the exact state of affairs when she arrives.

MRS. LUMB. An' a handsome dressin'-bag wouldn't astonish me in the least; not in the least it wouldn't.

[*Seeing that he has opened the bathroom door a little way and is peering in.*] What are you doing there, dearie?

COLIN. [*Withdrawing his head and closing the door.*] All right; that's tidy.

MRS. LUMB. [*With a shade of asperity.*] Isn't your bathroom always kep' tidy?

COLIN. [*Coming to her.*] Sorry; sorry.

MRS. LUMB. [*Who has finished laying the table.*] An' what are you going to give her to drink with her supper?

COLIN. Champagne; champagne. [*Pointing to the lower part of the cupboard.*] There are two or three bottles there—Paumier——

MRS. LUMB. [*Opening the cupboard, in which there are several bottles of wine and spirits and some siphons of soda-water.*] Two small ones an' one large.

COLIN. The large one; the large one, to begin with.

MRS. LUMB. To begin with! He, he, he! [*Putting the bottle on the table and making eyes at him.*] To begin with! Saucy!

COLIN. Oh, Mrs. Lumb, if ever there was a night for a glass of champagne——!

    [*The bell rings sharply and penetratingly. They stare at each other for a moment without moving.*

MRS. LUMB. [*In a low voice.*] That's her.

COLIN. [*With a fluttering heart.*] O-o-open the door.

MRS. LUMB. *You* let her in, dearie.

    [*She runs away into the bedroom and Colin, brac-*

*ing himself, goes to the door and opens it.
Lorna is outside.*

LORNA. [*Rather acidly.*] Oh, here you are!

COLIN. [*Beaming upon her.*] Y-y-yes, darling.

LORNA. [*In simple but well-cut clothes and carrying a handbag—entering and sweeping past him.*] Where the devil have you been, Colin? I was here half-an-hour ago. I thought I was bound to find you in.

COLIN. [*Closing the door.*] That hateful creature Miss Plant enticed me into her beastly lodgings. [*Advancing.*] Kept me there for ever so long. Much as I could do to be polite.

LORNA. [*Tearing off her gloves.*] Rubbish! Any woman can twist you round her little finger. They've only to flatter you—butter you up.

COLIN. [*Disconcerted.*] N-n-not at all, Lorna——

LORNA. [*Pocketing her gloves and taking off her hat and coat.*] You've had my note?

COLIN. [*Trying to assist her.*] Of course I—of course I've had your note——

LORNA. Get away; don't paw me. You see the nervy condition I'm in. [*Throwing her hat and coat on to the platform, then sitting in the winged chair and opening her handbag.*] Phew! Pacing the streets at the rate of ten miles an hour, all through your carrying on with Rosalind Plant!

COLIN. I—I—I assure you——

[*Mrs. Lumb comes out of the bedroom, shutting the door behind her. She has a big bundle of linen tucked under her arm.*

LORNA. [*Startled.*] Oh——!

MRS. LUMB. [*Softly.*] Don't be frightened, dear; it's on'y me. [*Picking up Colin's boots.*] Hope you've had a pleasant saunter.

LORNA. [*Powdering her face.*] Ha! Very, thank you.

MRS. LUMB. [*Going to the main door.*] Sech an interesting neighb'r'ood, it's admitted on all hands.

COLIN. [*Opening the door for her—pointing to the bundle of linen as he does so and speaking in an undertone.*] What have you got there; what have you got there?

MRS. LUMB. [*Whispering.*] Changing your sheets. [*Hoarsely.*] An' I'll bring you another piller.

[*She departs. Colin closes the door and turns to Lorna who is now using her lipstick.*

COLIN. [*Mildly.*] Yes, of course I've had your note, Lorna. Mrs. Lumb gave it me, with your suitcase, as soon as I came in. [*Drawing nearer to her.*] What—what—what—what on earth happened after I left you this afternoon?

LORNA. You may well ask. Anthony wound up the party by running amuck and almost murdering a photographer.

COLIN. A photographer——?

LORNA. A harmless photographer. Shattered his tripod.

COLIN. [*Incredulously.*] Shattered his tripod!

LORNA. [*Shutting her bag with a vicious snap.*] Previous to that he'd announced that he'll write no more children's books, and that he's busy over an illuminating work dealing with the late Queen Elizabeth.

COLIN. Oh, that's what he meant, then!

LORNA. Meant——?

COLIN. He hinted to me that he was on something different——

LORNA. And when I remonstrated with him, he shoved me against the edge of a table and bruised my hip.

COLIN. [*Horrified.*] Bruised your hip——!

LORNA. I believe he's bruised my hip—I haven't had time to look——

COLIN. Your hip——!

LORNA. And then he bolted indoors and locked himself in his study and left me to face the wreckage.

COLIN. [*Dizzily.*] Hip—hip——!

LORNA. [*Springing up.*] Don't! Don't! Don't keep on saying " hip, hip," as if you were calling for three cheers.

COLIN. The—the—the—the villain! The dastardly villain! The—the—the—the——!

[*They walk about the room in an aimless way, sometimes almost colliding with each other.*

LORNA. Ha, ha, ha! My reward—my reward this is, for all my patience and long suffering. A pretty recompense!

COLIN. A good job—a good job that he and I are three-quarters of a mile apart to-night!

LORNA. What I've gone through these last few months with his temper; what I've gone through!

Wicked deceiver! All the while his brain's been in a ferment over that wretched old Elizabeth!

COLIN. I hope I shall never meet him in the street. [*His clenched hands in the air.*] Lorna, I warn you, I warn you, never, never let me meet him in the street.

LORNA. She's had her turn in print, Elizabeth has. [*Beginning to snivel.*] If he must vary his work, w-w-why doesn't he write about the w-w-wives of m-m-modern l-l-literary men——?

COLIN. [*Encountering her in the middle of the room —himself watery-eyed.*] Oh, Lorna—Lorna—my poor —poor Lorna——!

LORNA. [*Weeping on his shoulder.*] Oh, Colin— Colin——!

COLIN. [*Holding her to him fondly.*] My poor, poor martyr—! [*The bell rings again.*] Damn! [*Looking at the door.*] Who's that?

LORNA. [*Getting out her handkerchief and hurriedly drying her tears.*] Wait—wait a jiffy——

COLIN. [*Motioning towards the bedroom.*] Hadn't you better go into the——?

LORNA. No, no, it's all right, it's all right. [*Brightening.*] It's only the children.

COLIN. [*Blankly.*] The—children——?

LORNA. [*Putting her handkerchief away.*] Thought they'd have been here sooner. [*With a little stamp.*] Open the door, Colin.

[*Staggered, he goes to the door and admits Betty and Brian. They also are carrying suitcases, Brian's being larger and weightier than his*

*sister's. Betty is in trim walking clothes,*
*Brian in another foppishly cut suit with an*
*ornamental waistcoat.*

BETTY. [*Passing Colin with a casual nod.*] 'Ullo,
Rembrandt!

BRIAN. [*Incommoded by his suitcase — sourly.*]
Evening.

LORNA. What have you been doing, kidlings? I ex-
pected you before this.

BETTY. [*Taking off her hat and coat.*] Brian was
such a hell of a time shifting his duds.

BRIAN. [*Letting his suitcase fall with a thud.*] Had to
hunt everywhere for my waistcoat. That cat Ellen had
put it in the wrong place.

LORNA. [*Sympathetically.*] Oh, my pet!

BETTY. [*Tossing her hat and coat to Lorna, who lays
them on the platform.*] Catch!

[*Colin comes forward, his eyes starting out of his
head.*

BRIAN. [*Sinking on to the chair by the round table
and handing his hat to Colin.*] Fagged out I am;
positively fagged out.

BETTY. [*Sitting on the fauteuil-stool and taking off
her shoes.*] You fagged out! [*Wincing.*] Oooo! Swap
toes with you anyway.

LORNA. [*Opening Betty's suitcase and extracting a
pair of slippers similar to her own.*] No sound
from your father, I suppose, children, after I left
you?

BRIAN. No, the Bolshie!

BETTY. [*Putting on her slippers.*] Unless you count his blowing his disreputable nose; I heard him at that as I crept by. [*Handing her shoes to Colin.*] Do they clean shoes here decently, Colin?

COLIN. [*Articulating with difficulty.*] Oh qui'—qui' decently.

BETTY. If they spoil those, my dear Velasquez, there will be trouble.

BRIAN. [*Wearily.*] What does Colin think of the nasty shock we're giving Child Man, Lorna?

LORNA. [*Sitting in the winged chair.*] I haven't told him yet——

BRIAN. Not told him——!

BETTY. We sent you on ahead to arrange things!

LORNA. Don't bully me, darlings; I'm so rattled. [*To Colin.*] We're going to read Anthony a lesson, Colin—a severe lesson——

BETTY. Scare him out of his senses.

BRIAN. His *senses!*

LORNA. When he emerges from that den of his, he'll find the house deserted—wife and children gone——

BRIAN. Vanished.

LORNA. Without a word or sign. Even our staff is in the dark.

BETTY. [*Between her teeth.*] Gosh! Shouldn't I like to view his façade when he realises that we've hooked it!

LORNA. We shall take pity on him and go back to-morrow——

BETTY. If he knuckles under.

LORNA. I've written to him to tell him where I am; he'll get my letter first post in the morning.

BRIAN. We're letting him off too lightly, *I* say. He deserves to be marooned for a whole month.

BETTY. Six, the demon!

LORNA. Stop it, children! The terribly unhappy night he'll pass—his anxiety—suspense! We don't want to be cruel.

BRIAN. *I* do, decidedly.

BETTY. And I. [*Doubling her fists.*] Jiminy, but I'm bloodthirsty!

> [*With an effort, Colin straightens himself, hangs Brian's hat on the easel, drops Betty's shoes, and goes to Lorna.*

COLIN. I—I—I see. [*With a ghastly smile, producing Lorna's note.*] Your—your—your note wasn't very explicit, Lorna.

LORNA. Explicit——!

BRIAN. Note——?

BETTY. What note?

LORNA. Colin wasn't in when I arrived, and I scribbled him a note and went for a walk.

COLIN [*Blinking at the note.*] N-n-not very clear.

LORNA. Gracious goodness, I couldn't write volumes on a piece of shiny paper, with a blunt pencil which that woman licked for me!

COLIN. I—er—I concluded you'd merely run round for a little while, j-j-just to talk matters over with me quietly. [*With a dazed look at the preparations for supper.*] I—I—I'd better ring and tell Mrs. Lumb we'll be four.

LORNA. No, no, no, we shan't be four——

BETTY. We shall only be two. Wake up, Titian; don't look so muzzy.

BRIAN. Yes, you and I have to sally forth and get a bed at an hotel, Colin.

LORNA. We can't all pig here; it wouldn't be nice.

COLIN. H-h-hotel——?

BETTY. There's one in Sloane Square——

BRIAN. And there's the Cadogan——

LORNA. [*To Colin.*] Betty and I'll share your room. I should feel so desolate in an hotel. And Brian will enjoy being on the randan with you for a night, won't you, Brian? [*Glancing at the supper-table as she rises.*] Not preparing anything special, are you, Colin dear?

COLIN. [*Shaking his head.*] N-no; there are only some cold scraps.

LORNA. They'll do for me and Betty. [*To Betty.*] Come on, Bet; let's go and spruce up. [*With Colin's help, she and Betty collect their hats, coats and suitcases.*] We *may* make ourselves at home, mayn't we?

COLIN. Rather! Honoured; honoured.

LORNA. If I wasn't so down in the mouth, this would be an awfully jolly adventure.

BETTY. [*Boisterously.*] A picnic! A picnic! What-ho!

LORNA. Betty—Betty——!

[*Colin opens the bedroom door and, carrying their belongings, Lorna and Betty disappear.*

224

BRIAN. [*As Colin shuts the door—rising languidly and strolling to the bathroom.*] I'll wash my hands too, deah lad; and then we'll take ourselves off. Came out without any gloves. [*Going into the bathroom and closing the door.*] If evah I forgive Child Man for this——!

> [*There is a short pause, and then Colin wanders away from the bedroom door and, coming up against the platform, seats himself on the edge of it with a woebegone face. Presently the turning of a key in the latch-lock is heard again and Mrs. Lumb, averting her eyes, puts her head in.*]

MRS. LUMB. [*Softly.*] May Lumby intrude?

COLIN. [*In a low voice.*] Come in.

> [*Mrs. Lumb enters, followed by Edith, a somewhat draggle-tailed servant. Edith, breathing heavily, is carrying a tray on which are the chicken, the pickled pork, the lettuce in a bowl, an uncut loaf of bread, a dish of butter, plates, etc. Mrs. Lumb is now overcome with bashfulness and Edith is equally shy.*]

MRS. LUMB. Take care, Edith. Another inch and you'd have had it against the door-post. [*Transferring the things from the tray to the table.*] We've brought the supper up, Edith an' me. [*To Edith.*] Hold it steady, my girl; don't woggle it. Haven't forgotten anything, have we?

EDITH. [*With drooping eyelids.*] Cheese.

MRS. LUMB. Cheese! [*Clicking her tongue.*] T't, t't,

t't! [*To Colin.*] If cheese is required, you'll ring, won't you, and Edith will fly up with it. Ring twice. That'll do, Edith. Remember, two bells are the piece of Cheddar next to Mr. Pollard's Dutch. [*Edith withdraws and Mrs. Lumb proceeds to put the various dishes in position.*] The chicken's a picture; all breast. Pity to hack at sech a bird. Young Crisp on the ground-floor ought to do a still-life of it, that he ought. Excuse the lettuce having a few brown specs, dearie. I hope an' trust they'll pass unnoticed. [*Squinting at the bedroom door and simpering.*] He, he, he! Lady in there, titivating herself?

COLIN. [*Slowly getting to his feet.*] Yes.

MRS. LUMB. [*Wriggling.*] Oh, don't!

COLIN. Yes, she's in there—with her daughter. [*Jerking his head towards the bathroom.*] And her son is in the bathroom, washing his hands.

MRS. LUMB. [*Turning to him with an expressionless face.*] I beg your pardon? Daughter?

COLIN. Daughter.

MRS. LUMB. Son?

COLIN. Son.

MRS. LUMB. [*Stonily.*] Small or grown-ups?

COLIN. Grown-ups.

MRS. LUMB. They—they've pursooed her, d'ye mean to say—run her to earth?

COLIN. No, no, no, no. Listen, Mrs. Lumb. Er—it's a little difficult to explain. There's been a misapprehension—a complete misapprehension. Er—I'm to blame; I'm to blame entirely.

MRS. LUMB. [*Stricken.*] Mis—misapperyension——?

COLIN. The—er—lady and her daughter are spending the night here as my guests. Her boy and I are going to an hotel. To-morrow they leave. I—I needn't ask you to forget what passed between us—between you and me—earlier in the evening? [*In a tone of entreaty.*] Eh? Eh, Mrs. Lumb? [*She gulps painfully.*] Thank you. And now—will you be kind enough to—to open the champagne?

MRS. LUMB. [*In a sepulchral voice.*] Who—who for?

COLIN. The two ladies. [*With the erect body and measured steps of a sleep-walker, she goes to the cupboard and takes out a pair of nippers.*] Thank you.

MRS. LUMB. [*Cutting the wire.*] Wastin' it, isn't it?

COLIN. N-not at all; not at all. [*Kicking Betty's shoes by accident and picking them up.*] Oh—oh, yes —these are the young lady's shoes. I shall be extremely obliged to you—and so will she—if you'll see that they're very carefully cleaned. Otherwise, I fear —to use her own words—otherwise there'll be trouble. And I shall be further indebted to you if you will show them both—mother and daughter—the utmost attention—the utmost—[*At this point Mrs. Lumb, having replaced the nippers, draws the cork. There is no explosion, merely the faintest plop.*] Thank you.

MRS. LUMB. [*Standing the bottle on the table.*] Flat as ditchwater. [*Regarding the bottle with a glassy eye.*] Like life. Like life.

[*She accepts the shoes passively and, still in a
comatose state, goes out, neglecting to close
the door. Colin is shutting the door when
Lorna and Betty come out of the bedroom.*

LORNA. It's getting frightfully late, Colin. Hurry up
and pack your bag, there's a dear fellow.

COLIN. Certainly—certainly——

[*He picks up the travelling-bag which is on the
chest by the main door and goes to the wardrobe where he searches for, and takes out, a
suit of clothes of a less dazzling kind than the
one he is wearing.*

LORNA. [*Advancing to the table.*] Oh, what a spread!

BETTY. Why, the man's a liar!

LORNA. Cold scraps, he said!

BETTY. A blooming banquet!

LORNA. [*Sitting at the table.*] It's a disgraceful confession, but I do believe unhappiness makes one
hungry.

BETTY. [*Dragging the fauteuil-stool to the table.*]
Simply ravenous *I* am; I could eat one of Colin's pictures.

LORNA. Oh, and look! Champagne!

[*Brian returns.*

BETTY. [*Sitting and seizing the bottle.*] Just the
thing for a growing girl!

LORNA. [*Cutting the bread.*] Have a glass of champagne, Brian?

BRIAN. [*Dropping into the winged chair and closing
his eyes.*] No, thanks, Lorna; I'll wait till later.

228

BETTY. [*Filling the glasses.*] I'll take my oath you will. You'll have none of this.

LORNA. Betty, how greedy!

BETTY. [*To Colin, who, carrying his bag and with his suit of clothes on his arm, is about to enter the bedroom.*]. Rubens! [*Raising her glass and drinking.*] Your health!

LORNA. [*Over her shoulder.*] Ah, yes! [*She raises her glass to Colin and he comes forward in acknowledgment.*] Your health, old chum. [*Drinking and then giving him her hand.*] So—*so* grateful to you for your hospitality.

COLIN. [*Bowing over her hand.*] Thank you, Lorna; thank you, Betty——

BETTY. That'll do, Van Dyck. [*Breaking her bread.*] Get on with the carving, Lorna.

COLIN. [*As Lorna attacks the chicken—gazing at her and the table wistfully, with a lump in his throat.*] Le poulet froid avec la salade de laitue!

LORNA. [*Shaking her knife at him.*] Now, Colin——!
[*He turns from them and goes quickly into the bedroom as the curtain falls. When it rises again the round table is laid for breakfast for two persons. On it are a pot of tea, a rack of toast, etc., etc.; and on a battered tray standing upon the fauteuil-stool, which is in the same position as when last seen, there is a covered dish. Edith is at the table in a dirty printdress and with her hair tousled and her cap awry. She takes the dish from the tray,*]

229

> *places it on the table, and raps on the bed-*
> *room door.*

LORNA. [*From within.*] Yes?

EDITH. [*Opening the door a few inches.*] Breakfast,
m'm.

LORNA. [*Out of sight.*] Thank you very much. I'm
coming.

> [*Edith closes the bedroom door, picks up her tray,*
> *and leaves the room. At the same moment*
> *Lorna comes out of the bedroom, dressed as*
> *before but looking pale and heavy-eyed. After*
> *a glance at the breakfast-table, she knocks on*
> *the door of the bathroom.*

BETTY. [*From within.*] Hullo?

LORNA. [*Raising her voice.*] Breakfast.

BETTY. [*Shouting.*] Sha'n't be long.

LORNA. Oh, do make haste, Betty. It's half-past ten.

> [*She goes to the breakfast-table and sits and pours*
> *out tea. Presently Betty enters from the bath-*
> *room carrying her sponge-bag. She is en-*
> *veloped in a bath-towel and is wearing a bath-*
> *ing-cap and her slippers.*

BETTY. [*With the air of a martyr.*] All right, if I
must be hustled! [*Tossing her sponge-bag on to the*
*platform and sitting at the table.*] But I'm not in the
least dry.

LORNA. Oh, Betty——!

BETTY. Give me a cup o' tea, for God's sake.

LORNA. [*Handing her a cup of tea.*] How many
hours sleep did *you* get?

HESTON & ISLEWORTH DIST.
HOUNSLOW
PUBLIC LIBRARIES

BETTY. Hours! Say minutes. A damnable night.

LORNA. I didn't drop off till daylight, and then it was from sheer exhaustion.

BETTY. No fault of mine; I tried not to kick you.

LORNA. Pity you didn't succeed.

BETTY. You needn't be disagreeable, Lorna.

LORNA. I'm dead.

BETTY. Wish I was.

LORNA. [*Sipping her tea.*] Tea's good.

BETTY. [*Sipping her tea.*] Hotter than the bath water, at any rate.

LORNA. I'm afraid I took the shine out of that.

BETTY. Selfish pig! [*Pointing to the covered dish.*] What's under the cover?

LORNA. [*Lifting the cover.*] Eggs and bacon.

BETTY. Yah! Don't show it me.

LORNA. [*Replacing the cover with a shudder.*] I wish *I* hadn't seen it. [*Taking a piece of toast.*] Have some toast.

BETTY. [*Taking a piece and pinching it.*] When was this made? Soft as putty.

LORNA. [*Nibbling her toast.*] Flabby as my old hat.

BETTY. [*Nibbling.*] Golly! Seems to me that that horrid Child Man's had the best of it, after all.

LORNA. [*Heaving a sigh.*] I wonder.

[*Eating their toast, they are both silent for a while.*

BETTY. Lorna——

LORNA. [*Staring at nothing.*] Well?

231

Q

BETTY. No deceiving *me*. I believe you were lying awake, not because of the noise of the traffic, but because you were worrying about your wretched husband.

LORNA. [*Turning upon her fiercely.*] Betty, I will not allow you to speak of your father as my wretched husband.

BETTY. Your adored husband, then.

LORNA. Callous girl!

BETTY. Fact is, you're as soft as this toast, Lorna, really.

LORNA. If you don't hold your tongue, I'll slap you; I will indeed.

BETTY. [*Rising.*] Safety first! [*Walking away, still munching.*] I'll remove myself from your reach.

LORNA. Yes, I have been fretting about Tony, if you will know the truth——

BETTY. Ha!

LORNA. I'm sure he's had as bad a night as we've had, and worse if possible.

BETTY. [*Sitting on the arm of the winged chair.*] Hope so.

LORNA. I've pictured every moment of it. The shock of finding we'd flown; his questions to the servants; the temptation to rush out into the street—to the police station; his pride restraining him; and at last his steeling himself to wait to see what to-day would bring forth! [*Rising and going to Betty.*] Oh, darling, what have we gone and done; what have we gone and done, darling?

BETTY. Done! Just what we intended; neither more nor less.

LORNA. Yes, but——

BETTY. [*Rising and flinging the remains of her toast into the grate.*] And all we have to do now—if a vile girl may give orders——

LORNA. [*Piteously.*] I didn't say vile, my pet——

BETTY. All we have to do now is to carry out our original programme.

LORNA. [*Eagerly.*] Go back at once? At once!

BETTY. Directly Brian turns up. March into the house with our heads in the air.

LORNA. Yes, yes, yes——

BETTY. [*Holding up her forefinger.*] Mind! No sneaking in with your tail down, Lorna!

LORNA. No, no, no; I promise. Run away and get dressed, Betty—— [*They hear the key in the latch-lock and turn to listen.*

BETTY. Here they are, I expect.

[*The door opens and Colin enters alone, carrying his bag and dressed in the suit of clothes he was seen to take from the wardrobe on the previous night. He also looks rather washed-out.*

COLIN. [*With an attempt at cheeriness.*] Good morning. [*Closing the door and facing them with a sickly smile.*] Good morning. [*Taken aback by Betty's appearance.*] Oh—perhaps I ought to have rung.

BETTY. Of course you ought to have rung. Lucky I'm presentable.

233

LORNA. [*Coldly.*] Where's Brian?

BETTY. Where's Brian?

COLIN. [*Putting his bag and hat down—obviously very uncomfortable.*] Oh, he'll be along soon; he'll be along soon. [*Coming to the breakfast-table—rubbing his hands.*] A'ha! Had a good breakfast, both of you; had a rattling good breakfast, hey?

LORNA. Colin——

BETTY. Where is my brother?

LORNA. What have you done with my boy?

COLIN. [*Weakly.*] He—he's a bit tired this morning —off colour——

LORNA. Off colour?

COLIN. We—we didn't get to bed till latish. He's dressing slowly—by degrees.

LORNA. Slowly——?

BETTY. By degrees?

COLIN. Thought I'd come on in advance. [*In response to a movement from Lorna.*] Oh, he's not ill. Give you my word he's not actually ill.

LORNA. [*To Betty—motioning towards the bedroom.*] Betty——

BETTY. [*Picking up her sponge-bag and going into the bedroom.*] Well! By Gum! This comes of putting your trust in Michael Angelos and such people! [*As she closes the door.*] Tell him off, Lorna.

COLIN. [*To Lorna.*] You said we were to go on the randan, Lorna. I recollect your very words—Brian will enjoy being on the randan with you, you said.

LORNA. [*Sternly.*] Where did you take him?

234

COLIN. "The Wish-Bone"; quite a nice club of its kind.

LORNA. Of its kind!

COLIN. [*Sitting on the fauteuil-stool.*] I'm a little tired myself. What sort of a night have you had, Lorna—you and Betty?

LORNA. Oh, delightful! Delightful!

COLIN. Glad; glad.

LORNA. I can't remember ever having had a more refreshing night.

COLIN. That's splendid.

LORNA. There are one or two drawbacks attached to this building as a residence, to which you must forgive me for alluding.

COLIN. Drawbacks——?

LORNA. Being near a corner, every motor-car that approaches it hoots like the devil.

COLIN. Yes, it has that disadvantage certainly.

LORNA. And the folks hereabouts are in the habit apparently of coming home at all hours.

COLIN. [*Tolerantly.*] Ah, well——

LORNA. And when they do come home, they're so fond of the fresh air that they hold animated conversations on the kerb for at least twenty minutes.

COLIN. I *have* noticed——

LORNA. You've a rich monopoly of lorries, too, I may remark.

COLIN. [*Becoming alive to her sarcasm.*] There *are* lorries——

LORNA. Which shake the place to its foundation.

235

COLIN. [*Rising.*] Lorna——?

LORNA. [*Wildly.*] And the milk-carts! The milk-carts! The entire milk supply of London passes through this infernal street. [*Throwing herself into the winged chair and rocking herself to and fro.*] Oh! Oh! Oh! The fool—the fool I've been to play this silly trick! A lot I shall have gained by it!

COLIN. [*Going to her—in an aggrieved tone.*] You appear to forget, my dear woman——

LORNA. I'm not your dear woman. Don't you dear woman *me!*

COLIN. You appear to forget the provocation you received—Anthony's brutality—your bruises——

LORNA. There are no bruises—not a single mark. If there were, I deserved them; I hit him first. [*Flashing her eyes at him.*] Colin Maccabe——

COLIN. [*Startled.*] Eh?

LORNA. [*Jumping up.*] The sight of you aggravates me. You look too ridiculous. It's more than I can bear —[*The bell rings.*] Brian——! [*She runs to the door and opens it, to find Anthony outside.*] T-T-Tony——!

[*He enters. As far as his increased age and altered figure will allow, he is very much the Anthony of the First Act. His clothes are old and shabby, his hair is untidy, his hat fit only for the dustbin.*

ANTHONY. [*Calmly, but with a face and manner full of grim determination.*] Good morning, Lorna.

LORNA. [*Looking him up and down.*] G-g-good morning.

ANTHONY. [*Advancing to Colin while Lorna is shutting the door.*] Good morning.

COLIN. Er—good morning.

ANTHONY. [*Turning to Lorna.*] I've had your letter. I've come round to ask you what your plans are for to-day.

LORNA. W-w-we—the children and I—are coming home, Tony. I—I'm just waiting for Brian; he and Colin have been sleeping at an hotel——

ANTHONY. H'm! [*Pointing, with an umbrella he carries, to the fauteuil-stool.*] Sit down. [*She sits obediently.*] You don't look very well.

LORNA. I—I've had a rotten night. And—and—and —and you?

ANTHONY. Oh, excellent, thank you. [*Waving Colin aside with his umbrella and seating himself in the winged chair.*] I had a capital evening's work after you all departed; the best of sleeping draughts for a literary man.

LORNA. [*Eyeing him in amazement not unmixed with awe.*] You—you've dug up some of your old rags, Tony——

ANTHONY. [*Nursing his hat.*] Yes, yes; my comfortable old garments. The relief to find myself in them again! Almighty Powers! the relief! The blessed, blessed relief!

COLIN. [*Annoyed at being " out of it"—dragging the model chair forward and sitting in a pompous attitude.*] Lorna has confided to me the events of yesterday, Gillbanks—what occurred after I left your house;

and, as a friend of long standing, I must say, I *must* say——

ANTHONY. Tscht, tscht, tscht! The less you say the better, Maccabe, on *any* subject. Don't interfere.

COLIN. Gillbanks——!

ANTHONY. S'sh, s'sh! [*To Lorna.*] Now, when you talk of returning home, Lorna, the question presents itself—on what terms.

LORNA. [*Meekly.*] Terms, Tony——?

ANTHONY. Conditions.

COLIN. Upon my soul, I should have thought that if a dictatorial attitude is to be adopted by either of you——

ANTHONY. Be silent!

LORNA. Colin, *will* you be quiet! Go out on to the landing, do!

COLIN. [*Rising and walking away.*] Really! Why not the roof? It was beginning to rain when I came in. Why not the roof?

ANTHONY. [*Transferring himself to the model chair.*] It must be evident to you, Lorna, that matters have reached a climax in our household, and that nothing but the most drastic readjustment——

COLIN. [*Sitting in the chair between the easel and the wardrobe.*] Ha, ha! A climax indeed!

LORNA. [*Rising and going to Anthony and putting her hands on his shoulders.*] I agree, dear; I agree——

COLIN. [*Muttering.*] Physical violence!

LORNA. And I propose that, to start with, we all

toddle back in a forgiving temper, letting bygones be bygones——

[*The bedroom door opens and Betty bounces out, in her frock.*

BETTY. If it's the smallest satisfaction to anybody, I haven't cleaned my teeth. [*Shutting the door.*] Forgotten my toothbrush!

LORNA. Betty——

BETTY. [*Discovering Anthony.*] Oh——!

LORNA. Your father——

BETTY. [*To Anthony.*] Hullo! Good morning. [*Surveying him disdainfully.*] My! You *are* dressed for Ascot!

LORNA. Betty——!

ANTHONY. [*Pointing to the fauteuil-stool.*] Sit down.

BETTY. [*Haughtily.*] I beg your pardon; you speaking to me?

ANTHONY. Sit down.

LORNA. Sit down, Betty.

BETTY. [*Staring at Lorna.*] L-L-Lorna——!

LORNA. Do as your father tells you. Sit down.

BETTY. Do as—he—tells me—! [*Slowly seating herself, open-mouthed.*] Here! I—I don't——

ANTHONY. [*To Betty.*] Your mother is proposing that we all return home together—return home in perfect amity; but before assenting to that line of action——

[*The bell rings.*

LORNA. [*Faintly.*] Brian—! [*Colin goes to the door and admits Brian who is carrying his suitcase and is*

239

*looking very yellow. He is dressed as on the previous night, but has put on his clothes badly. Lorna sinks into the winged chair.*] Oh, Brian——!

BRIAN. [*Indistinctly.*] Goo' mor'ing. [*Seeing Anthony and gazing at him in an idiotic way.*] Chil' Man——!

LORNA. [*To Anthony, as Colin relieves Brian of his hat and suitcase.*] Colin took him to a horrible club last night and kept him out of his bed till goodness knows what hour——

BRIAN. [*To Anthony.*] Y-y-y-your 'pearance is dishgrashful.

ANTHONY. [*Pointing to the chair at the round table.*] Sit down.

BRIAN. Wha'——!

LORNA. Sit down, Brian.

BRIAN. [*To Anthony.*] Si' down! May I ask the reason for this author'tive tone?

ANTHONY. Sit down.

LORNA. Sit down at once and don't argue.

ANTHONY. And try to collect your scattered faculties.

BRIAN. [*Lowering himself gently on to the chair.*] Don' argue——!

ANTHONY. I was just saying to your sister, sir, that before acting on your mother's suggestion that we all return home in a spirit of mutual forbearance it will be necessary to arrive at a clear understanding as to the future.

BRIAN. As to the—the f-f-fusher——?

BETTY. [*To Brian, quietly.*] Shut up, or you'll be sick.

ANTHONY. I don't disguise from myself that my reverting to my former class of work will ultimately result in some shrinkage of income——

COLIN. [*Wandering to the settee.*] *Some* shrinkage! Oh, Lord!

ANTHONY. [*Rising and moving towards Betty and Brian.*] You will both prepare yourselves for this change of fortune. [*Pointing his umbrella at Betty.*] You, Betty, will immediately set about taking lessons in typewriting and shorthand——

BETTY. [*Straightening herself.*] *Me!*

ANTHONY. You. [*To Brian.*] With regard to you, Brian, I shall see the manager of my bank this afternoon or to-morrow and consult him as to the possibility of obtaining employment for you in that direction. [*Brian slowly gets to his feet.*] I will not trouble you, in your present state, to express your views on the point one way or the other.

BRIAN. Excuse me. [*With a sweeping gesture.*] I have no hes'tation in saying that a commercial career in any shape or form would be partic'ly—par-tic-u-larily—obnoshus to me.

ANTHONY. [*Turning to Lorna.*] Lorna——?

LORNA. [*Gently.*] Leave it at that for the moment, Anthony. [*Rising.*] Naturally, the poor children are a little bewildered—knocked over——

ANTHONY. In any case, I shall have your support—your co-operation?

LORNA. Yes, yes. Ah, yes.

BETTY. [*Rising and showing her teeth at Lorna.*] Lorna——!

ANTHONY. We will go home, then.

LORNA. I'll pack up. [*Hurrying into the bedroom.*] Betty——

BETTY. [*To Brian, pulling him towards the bedroom —in a whisper, darkly.*] Brian——!

[*She and Brian go into the bedroom and Betty shuts the door. Anthony is putting on his hat when Colin comes to him.*

COLIN. [*Fuming.*] Pardon me, Gillbanks. I—I—I find it difficult to restrain myself. To put it mildly, your conduct, in my opinion, is not that of a sane person. You have utterly lost your mental balance. In short, you're a maniac. [*Dropping into the model chair.*] There!

ANTHONY. Oh, my poor dear Maccabe——!

COLIN. An out and out madman.

ANTHONY. [*Loftily.*] In throwing off the thraldom which has oppressed me for so many years! In heaven's name, why don't you summon up courage and follow my example; though I say it, my fine example?

COLIN. Your——?

ANTHONY. [*Walking about, flourishing his umbrella.*] Strike from your limbs the fetters that bind *you;* cease to be a humbug—a charlatan—a rank impostor. Give up your sort of quackery, as I am giving up mine.

COLIN. [*Rolling his head from side to side.*] Yes, we've had this out before, *ad nauseam.*

ANTHONY. [*Stopping to inspect the unfinished picture on the easel.*] Look at this daub—this crazy, ill-drawn thing! The emblem of mediocrity, my dear Maccabe; the emblem of mediocrity! Mediocrity in pictorial art takes refuge in the strange, the ugly, the bizarre, because it hasn't the strength to be beautiful. But better be a mediocrity, than a sham; better be an ordinary, commonplace artist, sir, so that you save your immortal soul. [*Returning to Colin and tapping him on the shoulder with his umbrella.*] Think it over, my good fellow. Even you must have a conscience, tucked away somewhere in your composition. Think it over and come and smoke a pipe with me soon—a pipe of peace.

COLIN. [*Rising uneasily.*] Er—Gillbanks——

ANTHONY. No, no, no; Anthony again—Tony——

COLIN. [*After a glance at the bedroom door.*] Anthony—I—I've a confession to make.

ANTHONY. Confession——?

COLIN. It—it—it—it concerns Lorna.

ANTHONY. Lorna——?

COLIN. When your wife came to me yesterday evening I was under the impression that she had flown to my arms as—er—as a means of escaping permanently from your—er—barbarous treatment, and I—I——

ANTHONY. You——?

COLIN. I was prepared to accept the situation and to offer her my—er—my protection.

ANTHONY. [*Indifferently.*] Ah? What about it?

COLIN. What about it! Good God, Tony, in face

243

of that avowal, don't you consider me a snake in the grass—a—a—a—a serious danger to your domestic hearth? Aren't you alarmed?

ANTHONY. Alarmed?

COLIN. Jealous.

ANTHONY. Of *you*?

COLIN. Of me.

ANTHONY. [*Laughing softly.*] Ho, ho, ho! Oh, my dear Colin, *you*! Ho, ho——!

COLIN. Gillbanks——!

ANTHONY. I apologise—I apologise——

[*Lorna bustles out of the bedroom, dressed for the street and carrying her suitcase.*

LORNA. [*Breathlessly.*] I'm ready. [*Going to Colin.*] Colin, I've been awfully cross with you, and beastly rude. I'm ashamed of myself; sincerely I am. [*To Anthony, as he takes her suitcase from her.*] Tony, Colin must dine with us to-night, and it must be a special dinner—a reunion—a regular jamboree. [*To Colin.*] You will, won't you?

COLIN. [*Stiffly.*] Thank you; I regret I have an engagement——

LORNA. Oh——!

COLIN. An important engagement from which it is impossible to extricate myself.

LORNA. Oh, Colin——!

[*Betty and Brian come out of the bedroom with a slouching gait and sour looks. Betty also is dressed for the street and is carrying her suitcase.*

244

HESTON & ISLEWORTH
HOUNSLOW
PUBLIC LIBRARIES

ANTHONY. [*Going to the door and opening it.*] Some other night—some other night.

LORNA. [*Shaking hands with Colin warmly.*] Next week perhaps, if not earlier. I'll ring you up. [*Turning to Betty and Brian.*] Now, children! It's no use being sulky and cantankerous. Away you go, darlings!

BETTY. [*To Colin—flouncing out.*] Morning, Tintoretto.

COLIN. Good morning.

BRIAN. [*Picking up his hat and suitcase and following Betty—to himself.*] Tahsome! [*Hiccuping as he disappears.*] Hic——!

LORNA. [*Going out.*] So long, Colin.

COLIN. [*Bowing—his hands in his trousers pockets.*] Good morning.

ANTHONY. [*To Colin—going out.*] Good morning.

    [*Anthony shuts the door. There is a pause, and then Colin runs to the door and reopens it.*

COLIN. [*In the doorway—calling.*] Lorna—Lorna——

LORNA. [*From a distance.*] Hallo?

COLIN. What time dinner to-night?

LORNA. Eight o'clock.

COLIN. Right! I'll come.

LORNA. Ha, ha, ha——!

    [*Colin slowly closes the door.*

THE END.